ARCO

THE
TELEPHONE
COMPANY
TEST

MARGARET G. EHRLICH, Ph.D.

MACMILLAN • USA

First Edition

Macmillan General Reference
A Simon & Schuster Macmillan Company
1633 Broadway
New York, NY 10019-6785

An Arco Book

MACMILLAN is a registered trademark of Macmillan, Inc.
ARCO is a registered trademark of Prentice-Hall, Inc.

ISBN 0-13-904244-X

Manufactured in the United States of America

15   14   13   12

Acknowledgments

In 1985, the officers of CWA Local 3204 and the Labor Studies Department of Georgia State University approached me to develop and teach a curriculum to assist union members to pass the Southern Bell Tech-TAB test. This liaison between the union and university sought to improve skills to benefit the corporation and the employee. It was our belief that the employee or potential applicant could improve their scores with test knowledge and practice.

In 1986, The Alliance for Employee Growth and Development, Inc., was formed as a cooperative venture between AT&T, the Communications Workers of America, and the International Brotherhood of Electrical Workers. Working with Kathy DeLancey, Regional Manager of the Alliance, I began to prepare AT&T employees to pass the BTAB test and other qualifying exams.

I wish to thank the hundreds of students throughout the USA that I have taught for their feedback and encouragement. It was for them that I gathered the material for this book in hopes that they could have a resource for passing these employment exams.

I would personally like to thank Morton Bahr, President of International Communications Workers of America, for his endorsement of this manual. I would also like to thank Jim Irvine, CWA National Vice-President, Gene Russo, CWA District 3 Vice-President, and all the officers and members of CWA Local 3204 for their part in making this publication possible.

For their invaluable support and patience during this project, I wish to thank my husband Jon and my family Jason, Ari, Susanna, and Shana Ehrlich. Jon's sense of humor is seen in the sentences for spelling words that he helped write. For his legal expertise, I wish to thank my confrere David Pollard. Thanks to my running buddy, Kindy Jones, for sharing the dream.

Thanks to my editors from ARCO, Jacqueline Urinyi and Jill Schoenhaut. Thanks to Lisa Bianchi for getting me started.

I genuinely wish you the best of luck in taking these exams.
Knowledge is power. Knowledge can eliminate fear.

Maggie Ehrlich
Honorary Member, CWA Local 3204

Table of Contents

Introduction

The BTAB or Business Telephone Ability Battery Test is a test administered to applicants of American Telephone and Telegraph (AT&T) as well its Bell affiliates. This test is given to current AT&T employees applying for job promotions or transfers. Temporary personnel are also required to take the test for appropriate job placement. It consists of the following four parts:

> Computational Facility
> Following Directions
> Number Groups
> Spelling Test

The *Computational Facility* test is a test of your ability to do basic arithmetic problems. You will have 9 minutes to answer 20 questions involving addition, subtraction, multiplication, and division of whole numbers, fractions, and decimals.

Following Directions tests your ability to carefully follow oral and written instructions. You have 10 minutes to complete 15 written and 10 oral questions. During this section, you are interrupted by a test administrator or recording that will give you additional directions.

The *Number Groups* tests your logic abilities to recognize numbers that are alike or different. You have 7 minutes to complete 20 questions. Four numbers are listed for each problem and you must decide which one is different.

The *Spelling Test* measures your ability to spell words correctly. You will have 12 minutes to answer 30 questions. For each question a test administrator or recording pronounces the word to be spelled and uses it in a sentence. The task is to select the series of letters from the answer choices that would be contained in the correct spelling of the word.

A BTAB Test marked Form C and D will have similar content but more questions and time. Form C and D has 25 questions for Computational Facility in 12 minutes, 30 Following Directions items in 12 minutes, 25 Number Group questions in 9 minutes, and 35 Spelling questions. Total testing time is approximately 40 minutes for BTAB and approximately 45 minutes for BTAB Form C and D.

TEST-TAKING TECHNIQUES

> *It is better to know some of the questions than all of the answers.* **James Thurber**

This book consists of a sample diagnostic test, instructions for all four tests of the BTAB, and five complete sample BTAB tests. After taking the sample diagnostic test you will be able to tell what areas you may want to review. Take one of the five sample tests after you review. Take as many of these tests as you need until you are satisfied with your performance.

You may not need instruction on any of the four parts, but still want to become familiar with the types of questions asked. You should find sufficient practice in the five sample tests. Take all the tests. Establish a strategy for test day. Will you guess? Will you try to answer quickly? Will you work all the problems you know and then come back to the difficult ones? Having practice tests to try out your strategies will give you a battle plan for the day of the test.

Work at your own pace in this book. Use this practice time to determine how well you reason an answer from the choices given. Treat this practice as a trial race. Once you are good at doing the problems try to increase your speed. Decide if you will work quickly to finish more questions or moderately for accuracy.

You have bought this book and you are ready to study but haven't studied since high school. What do you do? You need a study plan. Try using the The Three A's of learning:

Attempt -- Attempt to do all exercises and answer all questions. Make an attempt even though you may think you don't know the answer.

Analyze -- Analyze your errors and your strong points. Decide what caused you to miss a question and what you must do to be right the next time.

Act -- Act upon your analysis to prevent another error and attempt again, thus repeating the cycle of 3 A's.

Above all, practice. Set aside a time to work. Make test preparation a part of your schedule. Make a commitment to study and allow yourself enough time to prepare before the date of the test.

COMMONLY ASKED QUESTIONS
ABOUT THE BTAB

Here are the answers to the questions students most often ask about the BTAB.

Question: Will it be counted against me if I guess incorrectly? Should I only answer the questions I know?

Answer: No, you are not penalized for guessing. You are simply given credit for the questions you answer correctly. Each question offers four answer choices. You will have a one out of four chance of guessing the correct answer. If you don't answer, you have no chance of answering correctly. Each test is scored on the number of questions answered correctly.

Question: My answer was not among the choices listed. Is there something wrong with the test?

Answer: In a multiple-choice standardized test, one of the listed choices is the answer. If the answer you get is not a choice, re-evaluate your work. The listed choices often give a hint to the correct answer. You can eliminate those that are not possible choices.

Question: Is C the most common answer in a multiple choice test?

Answer: No. In today's computerized world it is easy to generate random sequences. Answers are equally likely for any of the choices.

Question: Is it true that *None of the Above* is never an answer in a multiple-choice test?

Answer: *None of the Above* and *All of the Above* are valid answers to test questions. They are not just place holders in multiple-choice questions. Always have an answer in mind before you look at the possible choices so the decision to choose *All* or *None of the Above* is an actual choice, not an alternative to a wild guess.

Question: I was told to work as fast as possible and not to worry about absolute accuracy. I would rather take the time and get a few right than to hurry and miss a lot. Is this a good approach?

Answer: Try to work as rapidly as possible without sacrificing accuracy. The more you practice the more accurate you become. Use your watch to time yourself where indicated. Get an idea of what a minute passing feels like. Mark questions that look time consuming and return to them when you have more time and have completed the less difficult questions. No one will question how you got the answer. You don't have to show your work or complete the entire question to get the answer.

HOW TO HANDLE TEST ANXIETY

Everyone experiences test anxiety at some time. Put this test experience into perspective. The BTAB is not a measure of your worth or success. Basically, it measures your test-taking ability. It is just between you and a place you want to be.

The contents are not that difficult. If test-takers were given all the time they wanted, everyone would do well and the test would not be a good screening device for job placement.

Here are some common questions about the BTAB with answers that may ease your panic.

Question: I'm afraid of taking the test because I haven't done well on tests like these before.

Answer: I won't bother you with cliches like "what's in the past is the past." Research shows that the more you take a test the better you perform. Familiarity, knowledge of what the test is like, and learning from your previous mistakes are all factors that should help improve your score. The more tests you practice taking, the more prepared and comfortable you will be when you take the actual exam.

Question: I panic when time is running out and I won't be able to finish. How can I prevent this?

Answer: Here is where a little test preparation can help you. Preparing for a test is like preparing for a race. You must learn to pace yourself and the best way is to run trials. Find out how much time you are allowed for a test. Look at the number of questions and decide how much time to allow for each. Practice the exams and record your timing. Learn to have a feeling for how fast you must work on each section.

Question: When I take a test, it really bothers me when I notice other people finishing before me. What can I do?

Answer: How do you know they are finished? Are you looking up? If so, you are wasting valuable time. You will have to find your place then read the question again. Most of the sections are 10 minutes or less and the whole test takes about 45 minutes. Surely you can concentrate and not be distracted in that time period. Rule of thumb: Don't look up until you have answered the last question or until time is called. The time you finish does not matter. What matters is that you finish all the questions before time is called.

Question: What do I do if I don't know the answer to the first question on the test? I'm afraid to look at the rest.

Answer: Go to the next question. The first question is the first experience you have with the test. The question may be confusing, but by moving to the next problem you may find yourself saying, "Now I know what they wanted in question number one!"

Question: I'm afraid I'll worry so much I won't be able to think or study, what can I do?

Answer: It is all right to worry about the test. In many cases a little worry can heighten your alertness. What you want to avoid is the panic that keeps you from reasoning or remembering. Sometimes the only preparation you need for a test is emotional preparation. Try to remove thoughts that cause anger, depression and lack of confidence before taking the test.

Question: I was cramming at the last minute and discovered I had more to learn. I'm considering staying up all night to finish studying. What should I do now?

Answer: Last-minute cramming is never a good idea. You should only save the last minute for *review*. Get a good night sleep before the test. Researchers have determined that it takes at least six hours for information to become a part of your memory. Lack of sleep will interfere with your ability to remember.

Hints to improve your speed or sharpen your ability to make an intelligent guess will appear in the instructional sections. You will find these suggestions in a telephone box similar to the following:

Suggestion: You can use your microwave as a timer. (Make sure the microwave is not empty) The bell will indicate for you to stop when the time is up. Do not use an egg timer. It is hard to set exactly on the number of minutes and you will get a distorted idea of the time allowed.

Now take the sample diagnostic test. Then score the test. Proceed to the section of instruction that you feel you need the most assistance with based on your score. Then take the practice tests.

PART I

Sample Diagnostic Test

SAMPLE DIAGNOSTIC TEST ANSWER SHEET

COMPUTATIONAL FACILITY

1 Ⓐ Ⓑ Ⓒ Ⓓ   3 Ⓐ Ⓑ Ⓒ Ⓓ   5 Ⓐ Ⓑ Ⓒ Ⓓ   7 Ⓐ Ⓑ Ⓒ Ⓓ   9 Ⓐ Ⓑ Ⓒ Ⓓ
2 Ⓐ Ⓑ Ⓒ Ⓓ   4 Ⓐ Ⓑ Ⓒ Ⓓ   6 Ⓐ Ⓑ Ⓒ Ⓓ   8 Ⓐ Ⓑ Ⓒ Ⓓ   10 Ⓐ Ⓑ Ⓒ Ⓓ

FOLLOWING DIRECTIONS

1 Ⓐ Ⓑ Ⓒ Ⓓ   3 Ⓐ Ⓑ Ⓒ Ⓓ   5 Ⓐ Ⓑ Ⓒ Ⓓ   7 Ⓐ Ⓑ Ⓒ Ⓓ   9 Ⓐ Ⓑ Ⓒ Ⓓ
2 Ⓐ Ⓑ Ⓒ Ⓓ   4 Ⓐ Ⓑ Ⓒ Ⓓ   6 Ⓐ Ⓑ Ⓒ Ⓓ   8 Ⓐ Ⓑ Ⓒ Ⓓ   10 Ⓐ Ⓑ Ⓒ Ⓓ

NUMBER GROUPS

1 Ⓐ Ⓑ Ⓒ Ⓓ   3 Ⓐ Ⓑ Ⓒ Ⓓ   5 Ⓐ Ⓑ Ⓒ Ⓓ   7 Ⓐ Ⓑ Ⓒ Ⓓ   9 Ⓐ Ⓑ Ⓒ Ⓓ
2 Ⓐ Ⓑ Ⓒ Ⓓ   4 Ⓐ Ⓑ Ⓒ Ⓓ   6 Ⓐ Ⓑ Ⓒ Ⓓ   8 Ⓐ Ⓑ Ⓒ Ⓓ   10 Ⓐ Ⓑ Ⓒ Ⓓ

SPELLING

1 Ⓐ Ⓑ Ⓒ Ⓓ   3 Ⓐ Ⓑ Ⓒ Ⓓ   5 Ⓐ Ⓑ Ⓒ Ⓓ   7 Ⓐ Ⓑ Ⓒ Ⓓ   9 Ⓐ Ⓑ Ⓒ Ⓓ
2 Ⓐ Ⓑ Ⓒ Ⓓ   4 Ⓐ Ⓑ Ⓒ Ⓓ   6 Ⓐ Ⓑ Ⓒ Ⓓ   8 Ⓐ Ⓑ Ⓒ Ⓓ   10 Ⓐ Ⓑ Ⓒ Ⓓ

Before You Begin

1. Have a timer ready for each section.

2. Ask someone to be a TEST ASSISTANT for you. A TEST ASSISTANT will be someone to call out the spelling words and give oral instruction to you. If no one is available, record the Spelling words with sentences, and oral instructions for Following Directions. Play the tape when you reach the Spelling and Following Directions sections of the exam.

After finishing, check your answers at the end of the section. Determine which section or sections you wish to review and proceed to the appropriate one.

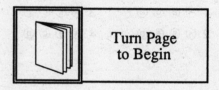

Turn Page
to Begin

COMPUTATIONAL FACILITY

Time: 5 Minutes. 10 Questions.

This test measures the ability to do arithmetic problems accurately.

<u>*Directions*</u>: *Solve each of the following mathematical operations. Mark your answers on the sample answer sheet.*

1. $1,435 + 2,023 + 879$
   (A) 4,227
   (B) 4,337
   (C) 4,340
   (D) 4,327

2. $8,306 - 8,279$
   (A) 123
   (B) 23
   (C) 127
   (D) 27

3. $3\frac{1}{2} \div 2\frac{1}{3}$
   (A) 1 1/2
   (B) 1 1/6
   (C) 1 2/6
   (D) 1 1/3

4. $12 - 2\frac{3}{7}$
   (A) 10 3/7
   (B) 10 4/7
   (C) 9 4/7
   (D) 9 3/7

5. 3.6×27.5
   (A) 29.72
   (B) 99
   (C) 92.5
   (D) 990

6. 35% of what is 18.2?
   (A) 5.2
   (B) 6.4
   (C) 52
   (D) 64

7. What percent of 95 is 24.7?
   (A) 23
   (B) 3.8
   (C) 38
   (D) 26

8. $.41 \times 8.2$
   (A) 3.362
   (B) 13.62
   (C) 328.2
   (D) 33.62

9. $12\frac{2}{5} \times 8\frac{1}{3}$
   (A) 36 1/3
   (B) 103 1/3
   (C) 96 2/15
   (D) 96 3/15

10. $13\frac{1}{8} + 21\frac{7}{9}$
    (A) 34 8/17
    (B) 105/8
    (C) 34 65/72
    (D) 34 8/9

STOP

FOLLOWING DIRECTIONS

Time: 5 Minutes. 10 Questions.

This test measures your ability to follow both written and oral instructions.

Directions: Use the table below to follow the written and oral directions. Mark your answers on the sample answer sheet. Caution: Avoid response errors. For example, if the correct answer is the letter "d" which corresponds to answer choice (B), you might make the mistake of marking answer choice (D). Be sure to mark the appropriate answer choice.

To the Test Assistant: Turn to page 16 for the oral instructions. If you do not have someone to read the oral instructions for you, record them yourself and play them back when you begin the exam.

	Column				
	A	B	C	D	E
Row A	1	2	3	4	5
Row B	4	5	1	2	3
Row C	2	3	4	5	1
Row D	5	1	2	3	4
Row E	2	4	5	1	2

1. Mark the number that is always to the left of 3.

    (A) 1   (B) 2   (C) 4   (D) 5

2. Find the number on Row B Column D.

    (A) 1   (B) 2   (C) 3   (D) 4

3. Mark the number that is always just above 1.

    (A) 5   (B) 4   (C) 3   (D) 2

4. All rows have five different numbers except which?

    (A) B   (B) C   (C) D   (D) E

5. Which column has the number two (2) twice?

   (A) C   (B) B   (C) A   (D) E

6. Add the numbers in Column E, what is the total?

   (A) 13   (B) 14   (C) 15   (D) 16

7. Which number is first and last in the same row?

   (A) 1   (B) 2   (C) 3   (D) 4

8. Which number occurs in two of the corners of the chart?

   (A) 5   (B) 4   (C) 3   (D) 2

9. How many numbers are in the chart?

   (A) 20   (B) 25   (C) 30   (D) 35

10. How many times does the number two (2) appear in the chart?

    (A) 3   (B) 4   (C) 5   (D) 6

NUMBER GROUPS

Time: 5 Minutes. 10 Questions.

This is a test of your ability to see how groups of numbers are alike or different.

<u>Directions</u>: *Each problem has four groups of numbers; three of the number groups have something in common. Darken the space on your sample answer sheet which corresponds to the one group that is different from the other three.*

1.	(A) 1022	(B) 1036	(C) 1024	(D) 1035
2.	(A) 1122	(B) 8899	(C) 3345	(D) 5566
3.	(A) 8880	(B) 7777	(C) 2222	(D) 3333
4.	(A) 3939	(B) 2626	(C) 1313	(D) 4848
5.	(A) 8024	(B) 7021	(C) 6014	(D) 9027
6.	(A) 1720	(B) 3229	(C) 2623	(D) 4542
7.	(A) 1107	(B) 1102	(C) 1113	(D) 1119
8.	(A) 4016	(B) 6018	(C) 3019	(D) 5015
9.	(A) 8067	(B) 5432	(C) 5431	(D) 5433
10.	(A) 1234	(B) 7654	(C) 3456	(D) 5678

SPELLING

Time: 4 Minutes. 10 Questions.

This test measures your ability to spell words correctly.

<u>Directions</u>: *For each question a test assistant will pronounce a word to be spelled and then use it in a sentence. Mark the series of letters from the answer choices that is contained in the correct spelling of the word. If you do not have someone to read the words, record them yourself and play them back when you begin the test.*

<u>To The Test Assistant</u>: *Turn to page 16 for the spelling list and corresponding sentences.*

1. The word you have just spelled contains which of the following series of letters?
   (A) occu   (B) ocur   (C) occuri   (D) ocurri

2. The word you have just spelled contains which of the following series of letters?
   (A) cency   (B) ciency   (C) ceincy   (D) siency

3. The word you have just spelled contains which of the following series of letters?
   (A) verment   (B) ouvern   (C) guvern   (D) govern

4. The word you have just spelled contains which of the following series of letters?
   (A) anse   (B) ance   (C) ster   (D) star

5. The word you have just spelled contains which of the following series of letters?
   (A) ckous   (B) cuous   (C) cous   (D) spik

6. The word you have just spelled contains which of the following series of letters?
   (A) law   (B) low   (C) lau   (D) lad

7. The word you have just spelled contains which of the following series of letters?
   (A) poncb   (B) bili   (C) billi   (D) ponci

8. The word you have just spelled contains which of the following series of letters?
   (A) plary   (B) pilary   (C) plery   (D) ptlary

9. The word you have just spelled contains which of the following series of letters?
   (A) nsends   (B) ncends   (C) scends   (D) scens

10. The word you have just spelled contains which of the following series of letters?
    (A) shious   (B) shous   (C) tious   (D) tous

[STOP] End of Test

For the Test Assistant

Oral Instructions for Following Directions

Directions: Wait 30 seconds after the test begins then read each question at one minute intervals. Do not repeat any questions. Stop the test at 10 minutes.

1. If you answered C for question number 1, change it to D.

2. In question number 5, change the word <u>column</u> to <u>row</u> and change the answer accordingly.

3. If you changed your answer to question number 1, change it back so that it answers the original question asked.

4. In question number 6, change Column E to Column D and change your answer accordingly.

5. If you changed your answer to question number 5, change it back so that it answers the original question asked.

Spelling Words and Sentences

Directions: Read each word and the sentence using that word. Pause 17 seconds before reading the next word to allow the test taker to answer the question. Do not repeat any word or sentence.

1. *Occurring* -- Heavy rains were occurring in the southern tip of the island.

2. *Proficiency* -- Proficiency implies mastery of a trade.

3. *Government* -- The government is providing food for the needy.

4. *Ancestor* -- The mansion was inherited from an ancestor of the Duke.

5. *Inconspicuous* -- The sign was inconspicuous, no one saw it.

6. *Laudable* -- Getting a college education is a laudable goal.

7. *Responsibility* -- It is your responsibility to study for the test on Wednesday.

8. *Exemplary* -- The model student displayed exemplary behavior.

9. *Transcends* -- He not only transcends himself in various ways, he also transcends his culture.

10. *Pretentious* -- The pretentious behavior of the executive secretaries alienated their peers.

ANSWERS TO DIAGNOSTIC TEST

Computational Facility	Following Directions	Number Groups	Spelling
1. (B)	1. (B)	1. (D)	1. (A)
2. (D)	2. (B)	2. (C)	2. (B)
3. (A)	3. (C)	3. (A)	3. (D)
4. (C)	4. (D)	4. (D)	4. (B)
5. (B)	5. (C)	5. (C)	5. (B)
6. (C)	6. (C)	6. (A)	6. (C)
7. (D)	7. (B)	7. (B)	7. (B)
8. (A)	8. (D)	8. (C)	8. (A)
9. (B)	9. (B)	9. (A)	9. (C)
10. (C)	10. (D)	10. (B)	10. (C)

If you answered fewer than eight questions correctly in any section, study the review provided before going on to take the BTAB practice tests.

PART II

Preparing for the

Computational Facility Section

Reviewing Mathematics

The Computational Facility test measures your ability to solve arithmetic problems. Each instruction section consists of examples and exercises for practice as well as a timed multiple-choice practice test. At the end of the review you will find a sample Computational Facility Exam covering all the mathematics review.

On the Computational Facility exam you will be given 9 minutes to answer 20 problems. No calculators are allowed during the exam. However, it would take almost 9 minutes if calculators were permitted! So obviously you need a little more than rote computational skills. You need to know how to reason and select the answer without using a pen or pencil.

USING ESTIMATION
IN MULTIPLE-CHOICE EXAMS

Sometimes you will be able to select an answer from the choices by estimation. When this is possible and you can select an answer without actually calculating, you save a considerable amount of time. Always estimate your answer before you attempt a multiple-choice math problem. This will give you an idea of what to expect the answer to be.

Rules About Estimation

- If the number ends in a 5, 6, 7, 8, or 9, round the number **up**.

  Example: In rounding 145 to the nearest ten, you would round 145 up to 150. Here you are saying that 145 is closer to 150 than it is to 140.

- If the number ends in a 0, 1, 2, 3, or 4 round the number **down**.

  Example: In rounding 274 to the nearest ten, you would round to 270. Here 274 is closer to 270 than it is to 280.

In rounding, if both numbers are rounded up the estimate is greater than the answer.

  Example: 27 x 35 = 945   Estimate: $30 \times 40 = 1200$

  27 + 35 = 62   Estimate: $30 + 40 = 70$

If both numbers are rounded down, the estimate is less than the answer.

  Example: 32 x 14 = 448   Estimate $30 \times 10 = 300$

  32 + 14 = 46   Estimate $30 + 10 = 40$

Use the answer choices to help decide what your answer should be. You only have nine minutes to work 20 problems. That's an average of more than two problems a minute. You must be able to analyze the problem and its possible answers. Many times the answer can be so evident that you won't need to work the problem at all! Just choose the answer.

Do as much of the problem as you can in your head before writing anything. Rewriting problems takes time.

OPERATIONS WITH WHOLE NUMBERS

Familiarize yourself with the following addition and multiplication tables. Use the tables to find the sum or product of two numbers. First find one of your numbers in the top row. Next find the other number in the first column. Move your finger down from the top row and over from the first column to the sum (Addition Table) or product (Multiplication Table) of the two numbers.

Standard Addition Table

+	1	2	3	4	5	6	7	8	9
1	2	3	4	5	6	7	8	9	10
2	3	4	5	6	7	8	9	10	11
3	4	5	6	7	8	9	10	11	12
4	5	6	7	8	9	10	11	12	13
5	6	7	8	9	10	11	12	13	14
6	7	8	9	10	11	12	13	14	15
7	8	9	10	11	12	13	14	15	16
8	9	10	11	12	13	14	15	16	17
9	10	11	12	13	14	15	16	17	18

Common Multiplication Table

×	1	2	3	4	5	6	7	8	9
1	1	2	3	4	5	6	7	8	9
2	2	4	6	8	10	12	14	16	18
3	3	6	9	12	15	18	21	24	27
4	4	8	12	16	20	24	28	32	36
5	5	10	15	20	25	30	35	40	45
6	6	12	18	24	30	36	42	48	54
7	7	14	21	28	35	42	49	56	63
8	8	16	24	32	40	48	56	64	72
9	9	18	27	36	45	54	63	72	81

TIMED WHOLE NUMBERS PRACTICE

Time: 7 Minutes. 10 Questions.

Now try working these ten problems under a time restriction. Use estimation where appropriate to save time.

1. 93+25+28+16+44

(A) 206
(B) 216
(C) 196
(D) None of the Above

2. 1090 - 878

(A) 222
(B) 213
(C) 212
(D) None of the Above

3. 896 × 708

(A) 643,386
(B) 634,386
(C) 643,368
(D) 634,368

4. 4266 ÷ 9

(A) 447
(B) 477
(C) 474
(D) 475

5. 28 + 19 + 17 + 24

(A) 87
(B) 88
(C) 89
(D) 90

6. 3723 + 14 + 936

(A) 4773
(B) 4699
(C) 4673
(D) 4763

7. 3021 - 447

(A) 2,574
(B) 2,547
(C) 2,573
(D) 2,584

8. 12 × 43 × 19

(A) 9724
(B) 10,703
(C) 9804
(D) 8904

9. 5063 ÷ 419

(A) 11
(B) 12
(C) 13
(D) 14

10. 4627 ÷ 7

(A) 662
(B) 646
(C) 651
(D) 661

Explanatory Answers

1. **(A)** Combine 16 and 44 to make 60. Add 60 to 28 and 25. Then add 93 for a total of 206.

2. **(C)** Your answer must end in a 2. You only need to do 2 steps of subtraction to know that 212 is the answer.

3. **(D)** Your answer must end in an 8. Your choices are C and D. Round your two numbers to 900 and 700 and then multiply. 634,368 would be the closest number.

4. **(C)** Your answer must end in a 4. Your only choice is 474.

5. **(B)** If you just add your ones place you see that your answer must end in 8.

6. **(C)** Combine 936 and 14 to make 950 then add 3,723 to get 4,673.

7. **(A)** Your answer must end in 4. Your choices are A and D. The next two subtraction steps will eliminate D.

8. **(C)** Try this fast method for multiplying by 12. Add double the number and then add it to the product of 10 times the number. For 12 x 43, take the sum of double (or twice) 43 and 10 times 43. 86 + 430 = 516.

9. **(B)** Round to the nearest whole number and divide.

10. **(D)** Your answer must start with 6 since all the choices begin with 6. The answer must end in 1 since only 7 times 1 = 7. Two steps of division will give you the answer.

Suggestion: Look for ways to check your answer by performing the opposite operation. In subtraction problems, pick one of the answers to add. There is less chance of error when you don't have to borrow. In division pick one of the answers to multiply.

OPERATIONS WITH DECIMALS

The most important rule to remember when adding, subtracting, multiplying or dividing decimals is to correctly place the decimals. This is done by lining them up when adding or subtracting, or by moving them left or right when multiplying or dividing.

Addition

Follow these steps to make sure decimals are lined up correctly: Write down the first number of the problem. Next, place decimals underneath the first decimal for every number in the problem. Fill in the other numbers of your problem carefully noting which numbers are to the left and right of the decimal. Your problem is then aligned properly. Add zeros at the end of decimals so that each number in a problem has the same number of decimal places.

Example: 456.87 + 567.8 + 78.9

1st Set up. Write the first number and decimals beneath	*Line up the other numbers. Whole numbers to the left, decimals to the right*	*Place zeros if needed and add.*
456.87	456.87	456.87
.	567.8	567.80
+ .	+78.9	+ 78.90
.	.	1103.57

Subtraction

The same procedure used in addition of decimals is used for subtraction.

Example: 345.1 - 65.892

1st Set up the number.	*Then line up the numbers.*	*Place zeros if needed, then subtract.*
345.1	345.1	345.100
- .	- 65.892	- 65.892
.	.	279.208

When working with decimals and whole numbers, place a decimal at the end of every whole number.

Example: 19 - 3.67

1st Setup the number.	*Then line up the numbers.*	*Place zeros if needed, then subtract*
19.	19.	19.00
- .	- 3.67	- 3.67
.	.	15.33

Multiplication

When multiplying by a decimal, perform the multiplication the same as a whole number problem. When you have an answer, count the number of places behind each decimal in the problem. That is the total number of decimal places you will move from the left of your answer to place your decimal.

Example: 4.5×2.8

First multiply	*Then count decimal places*	*Place the decimal in your answer*
45	4.5 1 place	12.60
x 28	x 2.8 1 place	<--
360		2 places
90	Total 2 places	
1,260		

Division

Just remember one rule in division for decimal placement. You must divide by a whole number. If the number you wish to divide by is not a whole number you have to make it a whole number by moving the decimal to the end of the number. At the same time, you must move the decimal equally in the number you are dividing.

Examples:

$24.82 \div .73$

```
        34.
 .73) 24.82
      21 9
       2 92
       2 92
          0
```

$20.272 \div 5.6$

```
         3.62
 5.6) 20.272
      16 8
       3 47
       3 36
          112
          112
            0
```

Decimal moves 2 places to make .73 a whole number and 24.82 becomes 2482.

Decimal moves 1 place to make 5.6 a whole number and 20.272 becomes 202.72.

TIMED DECIMAL PRACTICE

Time: 5 Minutes. 10 Questions.

Test your decimal skills with this sample multiple-choice quiz.

 Suggestion: Look at the total number of decimal places for your answer then look at your choices. Sometimes no calculations are necessary, just a choice of decimal place.

1. $3.41 + 5.6 + .873$

(A) 4.843
(B) 9.883
(C) 15.264
(D) 17.743

2. $.3 \times .08$

(A) .0024
(B) .024
(C) .240
(D) 2.40

3. $9.9 \div .33$

(A) .3
(B) 3
(C) 30
(D) 33

4. $125.25 + .5 + 70.86 + 6.07$

(A) 201.68
(B) 202.69
(C) 200.68
(D) 202.68

5. $1253.7 - 48.983$

(A) 1205.717
(B) 1204.717
(C) 1204.683
(D) 1204.617

6. 2339.88 ÷ 3.7
   - (A) 632.4
   - (B) 62.34
   - (C) 642.3
   - (D) 63.24

7. 1250.37 - 48.98
   - (A) 1201.39
   - (B) 1201.49
   - (C) 1200.39
   - (D) 1201.38

8. .06 × 7962.27
   - (A) 4777.362
   - (B) 477.6732
   - (C) 4787.632
   - (D) 477.7362

9. Divide 2339.88 by 3.7
   - (A) 632.4
   - (B) 62.34
   - (C) 642.3
   - (D) 63.24

10. 18 - 3.876
    - (A) 15.876
    - (B) 14.876
    - (C) 15.124
    - (D) 14.124

Explanatory Answers

1. **(B)**   Your answer must have 3 decimal places and the whole number is greater than 8. Your only choice is **9.883.**

2. **(B)**   Your answer must have 3 decimal places and end in 4. No calculation is necessary to choose **.024.**

3. **(C)**   Divide 990 by 33 for a quotient of **30.**

4. **(D)**   Combine in pairs then add. There is a total of two decimal places in the answer **202.68.**

5. **(B)**   No short cut. The answer requires that you borrow for an answer of **1204.717.**

6. **(A)**   When you round to whole numbers and estimate, your answer must be over 600 and end in 4. The number **632.4** is your choice.

7. **(A)**   Only two subtraction steps are needed to choose the answer of **1201.39.**

8. **(D)**   Your answer must have four decimal places and end in 2. The correct choice is **477.7362.**

9. **(A)**   No short cut. This problem is the same as problem number 6. Only the wording is different.

10. **(D)**   Think of it as change from $18 and add from 3.876 up to 18. The change would be **14.124.**

> *A man has 100 dollars and you leave him two dollars, that's subtraction.*
>
> Mae West in My Little Chickadee, (1940)

OPERATIONS WITH FRACTIONS

Definitions

- *Fraction* - A fraction is a ratio of two numbers. A fraction can have a value less than one (2/3), equal to one (5/5) or greater than one (3/2).

$$\frac{top}{bottom} = \frac{numerator}{denominator}$$

- *Equivalent Fractions* - Fractions with the same value such as 6/8 and 3/4.

- *Factor* - Number that goes evenly into a given number. Three and 5 are factors of 15 because 15 is divisible by 3 and 5.

- *A fraction equal to one (1)* - When a top and bottom of a fraction are the same, the value of the fraction is one (1) whole (8/8 = 1).

- *Proper fraction* - Fractions are called proper whenever the top number is less than the bottom as in 3/4. The value of a proper fraction is always less than one.

- *Improper fraction* - A fraction greater than one. When the top is larger than the bottom as in 5/4.

- *Mixed numeral* - A whole number and a fraction (2 1/3).

- *Multiple* - Products of a given number and another factor. The multiples of 5 are {5, 10, 15, 20, ...}. A specific number goes into its multiple evenly with no remainder.

Simplifying Fractions

1. *Reducing fractions to lowest terms*

This is a method used to divide and remove the greatest common factor of the numerator and denominator of a fraction. When the only common factor that a numerator and denominator share is 1, the fraction is said to be reduced.

Example: $\frac{9}{15} = \frac{3}{5}$

Both 9 and 15 share a common factor of 3. Divide 3 into 9 and 15 for reduced numbers 3 and 5.

These rules of divisibility of number 10 or less should help you in finding factors to reduce fractions.

#	A number is divisible by # if ...
2	it ends in 0, 2, 4, 6, 8
3	the sum of digits is evenly divisible by 3
4	the last 2 digits of the number is divisible by 4
5	it ends in 0 or 5
6	it is an even number and the sum of digits is evenly divisible by 3
8	the last three digits are divisible by 8
9	the sum of digits is divisible by 9
10	it ends in zero

2. *Making improper fractions proper*

The solution in fraction problems is sometimes improper. If this happens, you must change it to a proper fraction before selecting your answer. This is done by dividing the bottom into the top, getting a whole number and placing the remainder (if any) over the bottom as a final answer.

Examples:

$$\frac{5}{4} = 1\frac{1}{4}$$ 4 goes into 5 once with a remainder of 1

$$\frac{27}{5} = 5\frac{2}{5}$$ 5 goes into 27 five times with a remainder of 2

3. *Making proper fractions improper*

In operations of multiplication and division of fractions, you will need to change a mixed numeral into an improper fraction before calculating. This is done by making a new fraction whose denomination remains the same. The new numerator is found by multiplying the whole number by the bottom and adding the old numerator.

Example: $$3\frac{5}{6} = \frac{(3 \times 6) + 5}{6} = \frac{18 + 5}{6} = \frac{23}{6}$$

Finding a Common Denominator

Finding a common denominator and making an equivalent fraction is necessary for addition and subtraction of fractions. The collection of common factors to form a common multiple of two or more denominators is called the common denominator.

1. *Finding common multiples*

- To find the least common multiple of two numbers, find the multiples of the largest number until the smallest number goes evenly into the multiple. This common multiple will be used for your common denominator.

  <u>Example</u>: Find the least common multiple of 16 and 20.

  The multiples of the larger number 20 are {20, 40, 60, 80, 100, ...}. 80 is the first multiple of 20 that 16 divides evenly. Eighty is the common denominator.

- If one number goes evenly into another, the larger number is the common multiple.

  <u>Example</u>: Find the least common multiple of 2 and 8.

  Two goes evenly into 8. Eight is the common multiple and the choice for the common denominator.

2. *Making fractions equivalent*

Two fractions are equivalent if their values represent the same number. For example, there are several fractions having the same value but a different name for 1/2.

$$\frac{1}{2}=\frac{2}{4}=\frac{5}{10}=\frac{12}{24}=\frac{18}{36}=\frac{100}{200}$$

After you find a common denominator, you must calculate equivalent fractions with the new denominator. Equivalent fractions are found by multiplying your old numerator and denominator by a number that will yield the new denominator with a new numerator.

<u>Example</u>:

$\frac{3}{16}$ and $\frac{7}{20}$ $\frac{3}{16}=\frac{3\times5}{16\times5}=\frac{15}{80}$ You found that 80 is the common multiple of 16 and 20. Since 5 x 16 makes the new denominator of 80, multiply the top 3 by 5 as well.

$\frac{7}{20}=\frac{7\times4}{20\times4}=\frac{28}{80}$ Since 4 x 20 makes the new denominator of 80, multiply 7 by 4 as well.

Addition of Fractions

Think of fractions as units that you are adding together. One fifth plus 3 fifths is 4 fifths. When the units are the same you just add.

Examples:

1. *Fractions with the same denominators.*

    In fractions with the same denominators, you add only the numerators. In this problem the denominator is 5 and the numerator is the sum of 1 and 3.

    $$\frac{1}{5}+\frac{3}{5}=\frac{4}{5}$$

2. *Fractions with different denominators*

    Since the denominators are not the same, we have to find equivalent fractions for 1/5 and 2/3 with common denominators. The common denominator for 5 and 3 is 15. The equivalent fractions for this problem are 3/15 and 10/15. The sum is 13/15.

    $$\frac{1}{5}+\frac{2}{3}=\frac{3}{15}+\frac{10}{15}=\frac{13}{15}$$

3. *Mixed numerals with the same denominator*

    Add the whole numbers together and the fractions together. $10+11=21$ and $1/5+2/5=3/5$. Combine the whole number and fraction for an answer of 21 3/5.

    $$10\frac{1}{5}+11\frac{2}{5}=21\frac{3}{5}$$

4. *Mixed fractions with different denominators*

    Add the whole numbers 8 and 6 for a sum of 14. The common denominator for 6 and 4 is 12. The equivalent fractions are 2/12 and 3/12 for a sum of 5/12. The answer is 14 5/12.

    $$8\frac{1}{6}+6\frac{1}{4}=8\frac{2}{12}+6\frac{3}{12}=14\frac{5}{12}$$

5. *Addition requiring a carry*

    The sum of the fractions 8/9 and 5/9 is 13/9 which is improper. Change this to the proper fraction 1 4/9 and add to the whole number sum of 9 for an answer of 10 4/9.

    $$2\frac{8}{9}+7\frac{5}{9}=9\frac{13}{9}=9+1\frac{4}{9}=10\frac{4}{9}$$

Subtraction of Fractions

<u>Examples:</u>

1. *Fractions with the same denominators*

   The denominators are the same so subtract the numerators 3 - 1 for an answer of 2/5.

   $$\frac{3}{5} - \frac{1}{5} = \frac{2}{5}$$

2. *Fractions with different denominators*

   Since the denominators are not the same, we have to find equivalent fractions for 2/3 and 1/5 with common denominators. The common denominator for 5 and 3 is 15. The equivalent fractions for this problem are now 10/15 and 3/15. The difference is 7/15.

   $$\frac{2}{3} - \frac{1}{5} = \frac{10}{15} - \frac{3}{15} = \frac{7}{15}$$

3. *Mixed fractions with same denominator*

   Subtract the whole numbers for a difference of 2. Subtract the fractions 4/7 and 2/7 for a difference of 2/7. The combined answer is 2 2/7.

   $$10\frac{4}{7} - 8\frac{2}{7} = 2\frac{2}{7}$$

4. *Mixed fractions with different denominators*

   Subtract the whole numbers for a difference of 3. With a common denominator of 15, the difference between 2/3 and 1/5 is 7/15. The answer is then 3 7/15.

   $$8\frac{2}{3} - 5\frac{1}{5} = 8\frac{10}{15} - 5\frac{3}{15} = 3\frac{7}{15}$$

5. *Fraction from a whole number*

   You have a whole number but no fraction from which to subtract. Change 16 to the mixed fraction 15 2/2. Subtract for a result of 12 1/2.

   $$15\frac{2}{2} - 3\frac{1}{2} = 12\frac{1}{2}$$

6. *Mixed fractions requiring a borrow*

   Because 1/3 is less than 2/3, it is necessary to borrow before subtracting. Borrow 1 from 10 as 3/3 and add this to the 1/3.

   $$10\frac{1}{3} - 7\frac{2}{3} = 9\frac{4}{3} - 7\frac{2}{3} = 2\frac{2}{3}$$

Suggestion: The less writing the better. Try deciding the denominator as you read the problem. Write it on the bottom, draw a long line on the top and mentally calculate your numerators.

Example:
$$\frac{1}{5} + \frac{2}{3} = \frac{3 + 10}{15} = \frac{13}{15}$$

Suggestion: Try this quick way of adding and subtracting fractions that doesn't require getting a common denominator. Multiply the denominators.

$$\frac{a}{b} + \frac{c}{d} = \frac{ad + bc}{bd}$$

Cross multiply and add for the value of the numerator.

Example:
$$\frac{3}{5} + \frac{4}{7} = \frac{3 \times 7 + 5 \times 4}{5 \times 7} = \frac{41}{35} = 1\frac{6}{35}$$

Example:
$$\frac{8}{9} - \frac{3}{7} = \frac{8 \times 7 - 9 \times 3}{9 \times 7} = \frac{56 - 27}{63} = \frac{29}{63}$$

You won't have unreasonable numbers for which to find denominators on the BTAB test. After a little practice you will remember the ones used most often.

Multiplication of Fractions

Multiplying of fractions simply requires the multiplication of the numerator times numerator and denominator times denominator then simplify where necessary.

Example:

$$\frac{3}{8} \times \frac{1}{5} = \frac{3 \times 1}{8 \times 5} = \frac{3}{40}$$

Mixed numeral multiplication

$$3\frac{1}{4} \times \frac{3}{5}$$

Change the 3 1/4 to an improper fraction having only a numerator and denominator (13/4). Multiply 13 times 3 for the numerator and 4 times 5 for the denominator. The result, 39/20, is improper and must be simplified to the proper fraction 1 19/20.

Canceling

Whenever possible, you can simplify your product by dividing any top number into any bottom number before performing the multiplication. You can divide any bottom number into a top number or you can also cancel any common factors from the top and bottom. This simplification process is called canceling.

$$\frac{3}{10} \times \frac{5}{7} = \frac{3}{2} \times \frac{1}{7}$$

Before multiplying, divide the numerator 5 by 5 and the denominator 10 by 5. The problem is now 3/2 times 1/7. Multiply across for an answer of 3/14.

Division of Fractions

To divide fractions, turn over the divisor of the 2nd number. Apply the rules of multiplication of fractions.

Example:

$$\frac{3}{11} \div \frac{1}{2} = \frac{3}{11} \times \frac{2}{1} = \frac{6}{11}$$

Mixed number division

$$2\frac{1}{8} \div 1\frac{2}{3} = \frac{17}{8} \div \frac{5}{3} = \frac{17}{8} \times \frac{3}{5} = \frac{51}{40} = 1\frac{11}{40}$$

TIMED FRACTION PRACTICE

Time: 6 Minutes. 10 Questions.

Practice Addition, Subtraction, Multiplication, and Division of Fractions with this timed multiple-choice exam.

 Suggestion: Estimate the whole number answer in fractions. You may find the answer without any further computation.

 Suggestion: Before working the problem, decide if you will have to borrow or carry. Look at the multiple choices and pick the one that reflects one more or one less.

1. 3/4 + 3/8
    - (A) 1 1/8
    - (B) 8/9
    - (C) 1 1/2
    - (D) 9/8

2. 10 2/3 - 9 1/2
    - (A) 1 1/3
    - (B) 1 1/6
    - (C) 1 1/2
    - (D) 1 3/32

3. 3 1/4 + 4 1/8 + 4 1/2
    - (A) 11 5/8
    - (B) 11 3/4
    - (C) 11 7/8
    - (D) 12

4. 14 7/24 - 5 2/3

    (A) 9 1/3
    (B) 8 11/12
    (C) 8 5/8
    (D) 9 15/24

5. $286 \times 4\frac{1}{5}$

    (A) 1144 1/5
    (B) 981 1/5
    (C) 1201 1/5
    (D) 1201

6. $18 \times 8\frac{2}{9}$

    (A) 144
    (B) 148
    (C) 136
    (D) 116 2/9

7. What is the sum of 1/3, 2/3, 3/4, 1/2, and 1/12?

    (A) 3 1/4
    (B) 2 1/2
    (C) 2 1/16
    (D) 2 1/3

8. $3\frac{1}{5} \div \frac{2}{7}$

    (A) 10 1/5
    (B) 11 1/5
    (C) 10 4/5
    (D) 11

9. $12\frac{4}{5} \times 3\frac{3}{4}$

    (A) 48
    (B) 36 3/5
    (C) 36 3/20
    (D) 38

10. 8 1/6 - 5 2/3

    (A) 3 2/3
    (B) 2 1/3
    (C) 3 1/6
    (D) 2 1/2

Answers and Explanations

1. **(A)** The common denominator is 8. 6/8 + 3/8 = 9/8 = **1 1/8**

2. **(B)** The common denominator is 6. 10 4/6 - 9 3/6 = **1 1/6**

3. **(C)** The common denominator is 8. 3 2/8 + 4 1/8 + 4 4/8 = **11 7/8**

4. **(C)** The common denominator is 24.
     14 7/24 - 5 16/24 = 13 31/24 - 5 16/24 = 8 15/24 = **8 5/8**

5. **(C)** Change 4 1/5 to 21/5. Multiply 21 times 286 to get 6006.
     Then divide by 5 to get **1201** with a remainder of 1.

6. **(B)** Change 8 2/9 to 74/9 then multiply by 18.

7. **(D)** First add the 1/3 and 2/3 to make 1.
     The common denominator of the remaining three is 12.
     1 + 9/12 + 6/12 + 1/12 = 1 16/12 = 2 4/12 = **2 1/3**

8. **(B)** Change 3 1/5 to 16/5 then multiply by 7/2 to get 56/5 = **11 1/5**.

9. **(A)** Change 12 4/5 to 64/5 and 3 3/4 to 15/4.
     Each denominator will cancel leaving the product of **16** and **3**.

10. **(D)** The common denominator is 6. Subtract 5 4/6 from 8 1/6.
      Borrow 6/6 from 8, then subtract 5 4/6 from 7 7/6.
      The result 2 3/6 is reduced to **2 1/2**.

Suggestion: Think about what would be possible or impossible denominators? Look at the four choices for answers. There may be some that you can eliminate because they are not in simplest form or are not possible denominators for the fraction operation in your problem.

OPERATIONS WITH PERCENTS

Numbers in Percent Problems

There are only three numbers involved with percent problems. The percent, the part and the whole: a percent (%) is a part of a whole. You may have heard other names for these three numbers. The *part* is always the number in your question to either side of the word *is*. The *whole* is the number to either side of the word *of*. The *percent* number is always the number in front of the percent (%) symbol.

Table I: Similar names for percent, part, and whole

Base	Rate	Percentage
Base	Percent	Amount
Whole	%	Part
Of	%	Is

Solving Percent Problems

Because there are three numbers, there are only three possible percent questions that can be asked. In each problem you will be given two numbers and asked to calculate the third. Use this Percent Calculating "T" to solve all three types of percent problems.

Percent Calculating "T"

IS	%
OF	100

- Identify the two numbers given in the problem.

- Replace the words IS, OF, and % with the numbers from your problem. Remember, you will only have two of these three possible numbers in your problem.

- Where there are two numbers on the diagonal from each other, multiply them. Then divide by the remaining number. This method works for all three types of percent problems.

Example: *Given Percent and Part, Missing Whole*

Eighty-four is 30 % of what number?

84	30
OF	100

Eighty-four is near the word *is* in your problem. Replace the word *is* with 84. Thirty is the amount of percent, replace the symbol % with 30. Eighty-four and 100 are diagonal from each other so multiply 84 and 100. Then take their product of 8400 and divide by 30 for an answer of 280.

Example: *Given Part and Whole, Missing Percent.*

Forty-Eight is what percent of 64?

48	%
64	100

Multiply 48 and 100 then divide by 64 for an answer of 75.

Example: *Given Whole and Percent, Missing Part.*

What is 20% of 40?

IS	20
40	100

Multiply 20 and 40 and divide by 100 for an answer of 8.

Multiplying and Dividing by 100

Since the Percent Calculating "T" method uses multiplication and division of 100 you may wish to follow these two quick steps.

Multiplication: Move the decimal two places to the right and add zeros where necessary.

Examples: $12 \times 100 = 1200$ $23.5 \times 100 = 2350$

$.35 \times 100 = 35$ $.082 \times 100 = 8.2$

Division: Move the decimal two places to the left and add zeros if necessary.

Examples:

$$12 \div 100 = .12$$

$$3456 \div 100 = 34.56$$

$$3.25 \div 100 = .0325$$

Common Percents and their Decimal and Fraction Equivalents

You may find it helpful in percent problems to make some quick calculations by using fraction or decimal equivalents for percents. Use this table to make substitutions where possible.

Fraction	Decimal	Percent
1/8	.125	12.5%
1/5	.2	20%
1/4	.25	25%
1/3	.333333	33 1/3%
3/8	.375	37 1/2%
2/5	.4	40%
1/2	.5	50%
3/5	.6	60%
5/8	.625	62 1/2%
2/3	.66666	66 2/3%
3/4	.75	75%
4/5	.8	80%
7/8	.875	87 1/2%
1	1.00	100%
2	2.00	200%

TIMED PRACTICE WITH PERCENTS

Time: 6 Minutes. 10 Questions.

Suggestion: Determine the range of a possible answer. Is it above or below 50%? How does it compare to the answer choices?

1. 16% of 575 is what?

    (A) 85.3
    (B) 89.41
    (C) 90.68
    (D) 92

2. 135 is what % of 900?

    (A) 12
    (B) 15
    (C) 17.5
    (D) 19

3. 25 percent of 48 is?

    (A) 14
    (B) 24
    (C) 12
    (D) 16

4. 59.60 is 40 percent of what number?

    (A) 149
    (B) 1.49
    (C) 14.9
    (D) .149

5. What is 40% of 72?

    (A) 2.88
    (B) 28.8
    (C) 288
    (D) None of the Above

6. What is 2% of 29?

    (A) .0058
    (B) .58
    (C) 5.8
    (D) None of the Above

7. What is .05% of 150?

    (A) .0075
    (B) .75
    (C) 7.5
    (D) .075

8. 78 is what percent of 120?

    (A) 1.538
    (B) 65
    (C) 45
    (D) None of the Above

9. 29 % of what number is 476.92?

    (A) 16.4445
    (B) 16.4555
    (C) 17.445
    (D) None of the Above

10. 2339.86 is 370% of what number?

    (A) 642.3
    (B) 62.34
    (C) 632.4
    (D) 63.24

Explanatory Answers

1. **(D)**

IS	16
575	100

$16 \times 575 = 9,200$

$9,200 \div 100 = \mathbf{92}$

2. **(B)**

135	%
900	100

$135 \times 100 = 13,500$

$13,500 \div 900 = \mathbf{15}$

3. **(C)**

IS	25
48	100

$48 \times 25 = 1,200$

$1,200 \div 100 = \mathbf{12}$

4. **(A)**

59.6	40
OF	100

$59.6 \times 100 = 5,960$

$5,960 \div 40 = \mathbf{149}$

5. **(B)**

IS	40
72	100

$40 \times 72 = 2,880$

$2,880 \div 100 = \mathbf{28.8}$

6. **(B)**

IS	2
29	100

$2 \times 29 = 58$

$58 \div 100 = \mathbf{.58}$

7. **(D)**

IS	.05
150	100

$.05 \times 150 = 7.50$

$7.50 \div 100 = \mathbf{.075}$

8. **(B)**

78	%
120	100

$78 \times 100 = 7,800$

$7,800 \div 120 = \mathbf{65}$

9. **(D)**

476.92	29
OF	100

$100 \times 476.92 = 47,692$

$47,692 \div 29 = \mathbf{1,645}$

10. **(C)**

2339.86	370
OF	100

$2,339.86 \times 100 = 233,986$

$233,986 \div 370 = \mathbf{632.4}$

CLOCK ARITHMETIC

Clock arithmetic consists of adding or subtracting minutes and hours. All BTAB questions are based on a 12-hour clock.

When you add four hours to 3:00 PM, you end at 7:00 PM. When you add four hours to 9:00 PM, looking at a clock face, you see that $4 + 9 = 1$. This is because there is no 13 on a clock face. the clock has competed a 12-hour cycle and returns to 1.

<u>Examples:</u>

- If it is now 3:30 PM, what time will it be 1 hour and 20 minutes later?

    Add 1 hour to 3:00 PM and 20 minutes to 30 minutes for a result of 4:50 PM.

- If it is now 10:20 AM, what time will it be 4 hours and 25 minutes later?

    Add 4 hours to 10 and the result is 2. Add 25 minutes to 20 minutes for a total of 45 minutes. The time would be 2:45 PM.

- If it is 10:20 AM now, what time was it 3 hours ago?

    Subtract 3 hours from 10 hours for a time of 7:20 AM.

- If it is 1:25 PM, what time was it 150 minutes ago?

    Since there are 60 minutes in each hour, divide 150 by 60 to determine how many full hours are contained in 150 minutes. There are 2 full hours and 30 minutes remaining. Moving back from 1:25 PM puts the clock at 10:55 AM.

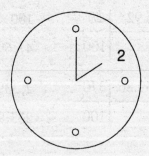

CLOCK ARITHMETIC TIMED PRACTICE

Time: 3 Minutes. 5 Questions.

1. If it is 150 minutes before 4 PM, what time is it?

   (A) 2:30 PM
   (B) 5:50 PM
   (C) 6:30 PM
   (D) 1:30 PM

2. If it is 10:55 AM now, what time will it be in 2 hours and 15 minutes?

   (A) 1:10 PM
   (B) 12:10 AM
   (C) 12:70 PM
   (D) 12:40 PM

3. If it is 6:15 PM now, what time was it 112 minutes ago?

   (A) 4:03 PM
   (B) 5:22 PM
   (C) 4:22 PM
   (D) 4:23 PM

4. What time will it be 3 hours and 28 minutes past 6:40 PM?

   (A) 9:68 PM
   (B) 10:08 PM
   (C) 9:08 PM
   (D) 3:12 PM

5. If it is 200 minutes before 3:00 PM, what time is it?

   (A) 12:20 PM
   (B) 11:20 AM
   (C) 11:40 AM
   (D) 12:40 PM

Explanatory Answers

1. **(D)** 150 minutes equals 2 hours and 30 minutes. Subtract from 4 PM for a time of 1:30 PM.

2. **(A)** Add 2 hours to 10 and 15 minutes to 55 for a total of 12 hours 70 minutes or a time of 1:10 PM.

3. **(D)** 112 minutes is 1 hour 52 minutes or not quite 2 hours. Subtract 1 hour 52 minutes from 6:15 PM for a time of 4:23 PM.

4. **(B)** Add 3 hours to 6 and 28 minutes to 40 for a total of 9 hours 68 minutes. The equivalent time is 10:08 PM.

5. **(C)** 200 minutes is 3 hours 20 minutes. Subtract from 3:00 PM for a time of 11:40 AM.

EASTERN   CENTRAL   MOUNTAIN   PACIFIC

Now that you have reviewed all the math required for the BTAB test, take this practice computational facility exam.

You have nine minutes to complete twenty questions. Some operations take more time because of the number of steps required. Addition and subtraction of two whole numbers takes less time than division or multiplication. It takes less time to do fraction multiplication than fraction addition where you have to obtain a common denominator before you add. Make a decision about the time required for each of the computations that you will have to perform. If you are pressed for time, move on to the problems that you know are less time consuming. Here is a chart with suggested ratings for speed of computation:

Speed Factors	3 Requires a lot of time 2 Requires average time 1 Can be done quickly

Section	Operation	Speed Factor
Whole Numbers	Addition	2
	Subtraction	1
	Multiplication	3
	Division	3
Fractions	Addition	2
	Subtraction	2
	Multiplication	1
	Division	2
Decimals	Addition	2
	Subtraction	2
	Multiplication	3
	Division	3
Percents	All three types	2
Clock Arithmetic	Addition	2
	Subtraction	2

COMPUTATIONAL FACILITY SAMPLE
ANSWER SHEET

1 Ⓐ Ⓑ Ⓒ Ⓓ   6 Ⓐ Ⓑ Ⓒ Ⓓ   11 Ⓐ Ⓑ Ⓒ Ⓓ   16 Ⓐ Ⓑ Ⓒ Ⓓ

2 Ⓐ Ⓑ Ⓒ Ⓓ   7 Ⓐ Ⓑ Ⓒ Ⓓ   12 Ⓐ Ⓑ Ⓒ Ⓓ   17 Ⓐ Ⓑ Ⓒ Ⓓ

3 Ⓐ Ⓑ Ⓒ Ⓓ   8 Ⓐ Ⓑ Ⓒ Ⓓ   13 Ⓐ Ⓑ Ⓒ Ⓓ   18 Ⓐ Ⓑ Ⓒ Ⓓ

4 Ⓐ Ⓑ Ⓒ Ⓓ   9 Ⓐ Ⓑ Ⓒ Ⓓ   14 Ⓐ Ⓑ Ⓒ Ⓓ   19 Ⓐ Ⓑ Ⓒ Ⓓ

5 Ⓐ Ⓑ Ⓒ Ⓓ   10 Ⓐ Ⓑ Ⓒ Ⓓ   15 Ⓐ Ⓑ Ⓒ Ⓓ   20 Ⓐ Ⓑ Ⓒ Ⓓ

COMPUTATIONAL FACILITY PRACTICE TEST

Time: 9 Minutes. 20 Questions.

This test measures the ability to do arithmetic problems accurately.

Directions: *Solve each of the following mathematical operations. Mark your answers on the sample answer sheet on page 53.*

1. $6372 \div 6$

    (A) 162
    (B) 1062
    (C) 1054
    (D) 1052

2. 20 is 40% of what number?

    (A) 500
    (B) 80
    (C) 800
    (D) 50

3. $\dfrac{1}{8} + \dfrac{3}{4}$

    (A) 7/8
    (B) 1/3
    (C) 1/2
    (D) 14/16

4. $\dfrac{9}{16} \times \dfrac{1}{3}$

    (A) 9/48
    (B) 1 1/2
    (C) 3/16
    (D) 9/38

5. What is 80% of 150?

    (A) 12
    (B) 188
    (C) 120
    (D) 1200

6. If it is 166 minutes before 5:00 PM, what time is it?

    (A) 2:14 PM
    (B) 3:14 PM
    (C) 2:34 PM
    (D) None of the Above

7. 3.801 + 16.2

(A) 3.963
(B) 19.001
(C) 19.803
(D) 20.001

8. 387 × 20

(A) 6640
(B) 7640
(C) 77400
(D) 7740

9. $8\frac{3}{4} \div \frac{1}{2}$

(A) 4 3/8
(B) 17 1/2
(C) 16 1/2
(D) 8 3/4

10. 540 is what percent of 900?

(A) 60
(B) 600
(C) 6
(D) 15

11. 8.34 divided by 0.02

(A) 4.17
(B) 41.7
(C) .417
(D) 417

12. What is 48% of 200?

(A) 96
(B) 960
(C) .96
(D) 98

13. 8014 - 256

(A) 7858
(B) 7768
(C) 7868
(D) 7758

14. 8.27 × 16

(A) 132.12
(B) 1321.2
(C) 132.32
(D) 13.232

15. $16\frac{2}{5} - 5\frac{1}{3}$

(A) 10 1/15
(B) 11 1/15
(C) 11 1/5
(D) None of the Above

16. $9\frac{1}{2} \div 1\frac{1}{5}$

(A) 11 2/5
(B) 7 11/12
(C) 7 3/4
(D) None of the Above

17. What time will it be 83 minutes past 2:45 PM?

(A) 3:08 PM
(B) 3:28 PM
(C) 4:08 PM
(D) 4:28 PM

18. 1080 + 202 + 22

(A) 1304
(B) 1282
(C) 1204
(D) 1242

19. 3826.1 - 1.65

(A) 2.21
(B) 3824.45
(C) 22.1
(D) 3.695

20. 95 is 38% of what number?

(A) 25
(B) 400
(C) 40
(D) 250

Explanatory Answers

1. **(B)** $6372 \div 6 = \textbf{1062}$

2. **(D)**

20	40
of	100

$20 \times 100 = 2000$

$2000 \div 40 = \textbf{50}$

3. **(A)** $\dfrac{1}{8} + \dfrac{3}{4} = \dfrac{1}{8} + \dfrac{6}{8} = \dfrac{\textbf{7}}{\textbf{8}}$

4. **(C)** $\dfrac{9}{16} \times \dfrac{1}{3} = \dfrac{\textbf{3}}{\textbf{16}}$

5. **(C)**

is	80
150	100

$150 \times 80 = 12,000$

$12,000 \div 100 = \textbf{120}$

6. **(A)** 166 minutes is 2 hours and 46 minutes.
   Subtract from 5 PM for a time of **2:14 PM.**

7. **(D)**
$$\begin{array}{r} 3.801 \\ + 16.2 \\ \hline \textbf{20.001} \end{array}$$

8. **(D)** $387 \times 20 = \textbf{7,740}$

9. **(B)** $\dfrac{35}{4} \times \dfrac{2}{1} = \dfrac{35}{2} = \textbf{17}\dfrac{\textbf{1}}{\textbf{2}}$

10. **(A)**

540	%
900	100

$540 \times 100 = 54,000$

$54,000 \div 900 = \textbf{60}$

11. **(D)** $8.34 \div .02 = \textbf{417}$

12. **(A)**

IS	48
200	100

$48 \times 200 = 9600$

$9600 \div 100 = \mathbf{96}$

13. **(D)** $8014 - 256 = \mathbf{7758}$

14. **(C)**

$$\begin{array}{r} 8.27 \\ \underline{1.6} \\ 4962 \\ \underline{827} \\ \mathbf{13.232} \end{array}$$

15. **(B)** $16\dfrac{6}{15} - 5\dfrac{5}{15} = \mathbf{11\dfrac{1}{15}}$

16. **(B)** $\dfrac{19}{2} \times \dfrac{5}{6} = \dfrac{95}{12} = \mathbf{7\dfrac{11}{12}}$

17. **(C)**   83 minutes is 1 hour and 23 minutes.
Add this to 2:45 for a time of 3 hours 68 minutes or **4:08 PM.**

18. **(A)**   Combine 202 and 22 for a total of 224 then add to 1,080 for a sum of **1304.**

19. **(B)**

$$\begin{array}{r} 38.60 \\ \underline{-\ 1.65} \\ \mathbf{36.95} \end{array}$$

20. **(D)**

95	38
of	100

$95 \times 100 = 9500$

$9500 \div 38 = \mathbf{250}$

PART III

Preparing for the

Following Directions Section

Written Instructions

The Following Directions portion of the exam will consist of a table with rows and columns similar to the one below.

| | Column | | | |
	A	B	C	D
Row A	1	2	3	4
Row B	2	3	1	4
Row C	3	4	2	1
Row D	2	4	1	2

Letters, numbers, or both may appear in this chart. You will be asked written questions similar to the following:

1. What is the number in Row A Column B?

   At the intersection of Row A and Column B you find the number 2. Your answer is 2.

2. What number is always below the number 1?

   Find the number one in every place that it occurs in the chart. There are four ones: Row A Column A, Row B Column C, Row C Column D, and Row D Column C. Check each number below. The answer is 2.

3. In Row C, what follows 2?

   The number 2 in Column C is in Row C. It has the number 1 after it. The answer is 1.

4. The 4 in Row C is just below which number?

   Find the number 4 in Row C and Column B. The number 3 is below.

5. If Row D were reversed, what number would follow 1?

   Reversed in this question means backwards. The order of numbers for Row D are now 2,1,4,2. The number after 1 is 4.

6. What is the sum of numbers in Row A equal to?

   Add all the numbers in Row A (3,4,2,1) for a total of 10.

7. The sum of numbers in Column A is equal to?

   Add all the numbers in Column A (1,2,3,2) for a total of 8.

8. Reverse Row B. What number is now in Row B Column C?

   The order of Row B is now 4,1,3,2. The number 3 is in Column C.

9. Reverse Column C and D. What number is now in Row C Column D?

   The reverse of Column C is not necessary to answer this problem. Column D reversed has a new order of 2,1,4,4. The answer is 4.

10. What is the sum of the numbers in Row A and Column A?

    The answer is 17. Don't count the 1 in Row A and Column A twice.

 Suggestion: Find the reference position. It is usually the location given at the end of the question.   From this position you can only move in 4 directions, ABOVE (A), BELOW (B), LEFT (L), or RIGHT (R). Make short hand notes of the direction as you read each question.

Some questions will involve multiple instructions similar to the ones below:

1. What number is to the *right* of the number *above* the number in Row C Column B?

   As you read question 1 make notes of the position. R then A. Find your reference position at Row C Column B. This is the number 4. Next move above to the number 3. Now right to 1 in Row B Column C. The number 1 is your answer.

2. Reverse Row C. What number is below the number to the right of the number below the number in Row A Column C?

   First reverse Row C. This makes the order of Row C 1,2,4,3. Making notes from the directions given you should have **B R B**. Find the number now in Row A Column C. This is the number 3. From this number move below to 1 in Row B Column C, to the right to 4 in Row 3 B Column D, then below again to 4 in Row C Column D. The answer is 3.

Written Instructions Practice Exercise

Directions: Answer the following questions using the chart on page 63.

1. What is the number in Row B Column C?

2. What number is most often above 2?

3. In Row C, what comes before 1?

4. If Column D was reversed, what number would follow 1?

5. The 3 in Row C is just above what number?

6. The sum of the numbers in Column C is equal to?

7. The sum of numbers in Column A and Row B are equal to?

8. Reverse Column A. What number is now in Column A Row C?

9. Reverse Column A then Row D. What number is now in Column A Row D?

10. How many different numbers are in Row D?

11. What number is to the left of the number above the number in Row D Column C?

12. Reverse Column D. What number is 2 spaces to the right of the number above the number in Row D Column B?

Answers

1. (1)	4. (4)	7. (16)	10. (3)
2. (1)	5. (2)	8. (2)	11. (4)
3. (2)	6. (7)	9. (2)	12. (4)

Suggestion: Avoid response errors. For example, if the correct answer is the letter "d" which corresponds to answer choice (B), you might make the mistake of marking answer choice (D). Be sure to mark the appropriate answer choice.

Oral Instructions

While answering the written questions for the Following Directions test, you will also be given oral instructions. These instructions may be administered by a Test Assistant or they may be prerecorded and you will hear them over headphones from a tape. One instruction will be given every minute for ten minutes similar to the following.

1. If you answered A for Question number 1, change it to B.

    Check to see if you answered A. If so change to B. If you did not answer A, no change is necessary.

2. Change Row C to Row B in Question number 5. Change your answer accordingly.

    Reread question number 5 with the replacement of Row B for Row C. The 4 in Row B is just below the 4 in Row A. Change your original answer of 3 to 4.

3. Change Column A to Column B in question number 7. Change your answer accordingly.

    The question would now be to add the numbers in Column B. This total is 13. You would replace your original answer of 8 with 13.

4. If you changed your answer to number 1, change it back so it answers the original question.

    If you changed the answer to question 1 to B after the first oral instruction, change the answer back to A.

If a previous oral instruction caused you to change an answer, sometimes you will be instructed to change it back. It may seem frustrating to change answers back and forth. Remember, you are being tested on how well you follow directions with interruptions, and how quickly you can return to your work.

HANDLING INTERRUPTIONS

When an oral instruction is given, stop where you are immediately to hear the instruction. Make notes of the instructions, you will only hear them once. You will not have a chance to ask for a repeat of the question or ask "What did you say?"

It is natural to look up when you hear an instruction. However, this can cause you to lose your place and you will waste time trying to reestablish your position. It is helpful to take a ruler or piece of paper and slide it over each of the questions as you complete them. After you hear the oral instruction your eyes will automatically return to the last place you were working.

Sometimes you will be asked to change an answer and then another instruction will tell you to change it back. Lightly erase the old choice so that when this happens you can see the old answer and will not have to reread the problem to correctly change the answer. When you arrive at your final answer make sure it is the only one clearly marked.

Pacing yourself will be easy in this section. There are ten oral instructions and each is given at a one minute interval. You can keep tally of the questions and know exactly how much time you have used.

Now try the following multiple choice timed exam in following directions. You will need someone to read the oral instructions to you as you take the test.

FOLLOWING DIRECTIONS SAMPLE
ANSWER SHEET

1 Ⓐ Ⓑ Ⓒ Ⓓ   6 Ⓐ Ⓑ Ⓒ Ⓓ   11 Ⓐ Ⓑ Ⓒ Ⓓ

2 Ⓐ Ⓑ Ⓒ Ⓓ   7 Ⓐ Ⓑ Ⓒ Ⓓ   12 Ⓐ Ⓑ Ⓒ Ⓓ

3 Ⓐ Ⓑ Ⓒ Ⓓ   8 Ⓐ Ⓑ Ⓒ Ⓓ   13 Ⓐ Ⓑ Ⓒ Ⓓ

4 Ⓐ Ⓑ Ⓒ Ⓓ   9 Ⓐ Ⓑ Ⓒ Ⓓ   14 Ⓐ Ⓑ Ⓒ Ⓓ

5 Ⓐ Ⓑ Ⓒ Ⓓ   10 Ⓐ Ⓑ Ⓒ Ⓓ   15 Ⓐ Ⓑ Ⓒ Ⓓ

FOLLOWING DIRECTIONS PRACTICE TEST

Time: 10 Minutes. 15 Questions.

To the Test Assistant: Turn to page 73 for the oral instructions. If you do not have someone to read the oral directions for you, record them yourself and play them back when you begin the exam.

	Column A	Column B	Column C	Column D
Row A	M	N	P	Q
Row B	Q	M	O	R
Row C	N	R	P	M
Row D	O	Q	M	P
Row E	P	O	R	N

1. Which letter appears in Row E, Column B?

   (A) M   (B) O   (C) P   (D) R

2. What letter is to the right of the letter in Row C, Column C?

   (A) P   (B) R   (C) O   (D) M

3. What letter is above the letter in Column B, Row D?

   (A) R   (B) Q   (C) N   (D) P

4. What letter does not appear in the table?

   (A) M   (B) O   (C) W   (D) Q

5. How many times does the letter M appear in the table?

   (A) 4   (B) 3   (C) 7   (D) 5

6. Reverse Column A and C. What letter is to the right of the letter in Column B, Row D?

   (A) M   (B) O   (C) P   (D) R

7. If Row D were reversed, what letter would be just above the letter just above the letter to the right of the letter M?

   (A) M   (B) Q   (C) R   (D) O

8. What letter is 2 spaces to the left of the letter that is just above the letter next to the last letter in Row C?

   (A) M   (B) N   (C) O   (D) Q

9. If Column A, B, and D were reversed, which row would contain the most M's?

   (A) B   (B) C   (C) D   (D) E

10. What letter is to the left of the letter that is two spaces below the letter that is to the right of the first letter in the table?

    (A) P   (B) N   (C) M   (D) Q

11. What letter is 2 spaces below the letter to the right of the letter in Column B, Row C?

    (A) R   (B) P   (C) N   (D) M

12. In Row D, what letter is to the left of Q?

    (A) P   (B) M   (C) O   (D) N

13. In Columns B and C what letter is always below M?

    (A) R   (B) O   (C) P   (D) Q

14. If Column B was reversed, what would be below the letter R?

    (A) O   (B) N   (C) M   (D) P

15. How many different letters are in Row C and Column D?

    (A) 8   (B) 9   (C) 4   (D) 5

Oral Instruction

To the Test Assistant: Wait 30 seconds after the test begins then read each question at one minute intervals. Do not repeat any questions. Stop the test at 10 minutes.

1. If you answered C for question number 1, change it to D.

2. Change Column B to Column C in Question number 3. Change your answer if necessary.

3. If you answered A in question number 5, change it to C.

4. Change Row C to Row D in question number 8. Change your answer if necessary.

5. If you changed your answer to question number 3, change it to answer the original question.

6. If you answered B for question number 10, change it to C.

7. In question number 7, change Row D to its original order and answer the question accordingly.

8. If you answered C for question number 12, change it to A.

9. If you changed your answer to C in question number 10, change it to answer the original question.

10. Change the letter R to the letter M in question number 14 and answer the question accordingly.

Answers

1. B	4. C	7. C	10. B	13. A
2. D	5. C	8. B	11. A	14. B
3. A	6. B	9 C	12. A	15. D

PART IV

Preparing for the

Number Groups Section

Identifying Different Number Groups

To select which group of numbers is different from the other three sets, you must determine how the others are alike.

There are two approaches to analyze how these groups are alike. First you must know *what* to look for and then consider *how* to look at the four sets of numbers to establish a pattern.

What you should look for

- *even or odd numbers*

    1.   8673   8672   8679   8675

    Even numbers end in 2, 4, 6, 8, or 0. Odd number end in 1, 3, 5, 7, or 9. 8672 is different in this group because it is an even number. The other three groups are odd numbers 3, 9, 5.

    2.   456   454   455   458

    455 is different in this group because it is an odd number. The other three groups are even numbers.

- *differences or sums of numbers*

    1.   6511   7815   4811   4913

    In this group the 1st number plus the 2nd is equal to the last two numbers. 4811 is different because $4 + 8 = 12$, not 11.

    2.   1134   3060   3222   7102

    These three numbers have a common sum. The sum of the digits of each number is equal to nine. 7102 is different because the digits $7 + 1 + 0 + 2 = 10$, not nine.

    3.   385   187   397   451

    The sum of the first and last digit equals the middle number. 397 is different because $3 + 7$ does not equal 9.

• *multiplication or division of numbers*

1. 4520 4728 6848 3416

Here the product of the first two numbers equals to the last two numbers. 3416 is different because 3 x 4 = 12, not 16.

2. 213 497 357 639

The last number multiplied by 7 equals the first pair of digits. 357 is different because 7 multiplied by 7 equals 49, not 35.

• *consecutive ascending and descending numbers*

1. 2345 3457 5678 1234

3457 is different because it does not ascend consecutively. If the number had been 3456, it would have followed the ascending pattern of the other three groups.

2. 9876 7654 6432 5432

6432 is different because it does not descend consecutively. If this number had been 6543, it would have followed the descending pattern of the other three groups.

• *different arrangements of the same digits*

5783 3587 8735 5893

The numbers 5783, 3587, and 8735 are all different arrangements of the numbers 5, 7, 8, and 3. The number 5893 contains the different number 9.

• *repeats*

1111 3333 4447 5555

The number 4447 is different because it does not have 4 identical numbers.

Suggestion: Trust your instinct. Sometimes you will just know a group is different by the way it looks with the other numbers. By all means, guess and choose an answer for all 20 problems.

How to look

- *whole*

2222	4444	5556	6666

To determine the repeating pattern, you must look at all 4 numbers at once. 5556 is different.

- *part*

Consider the four digit number in two parts consisting of the first and second pair of numbers.

1.   4520   4728   6848   3416

The product of the first pair of digits equals the last pair of numbers. 3416 is different because the first pair (34) 3 times 4 does not equal the last pair 16.

2.   4550   5055   3742   5357

Subtract the first pair from the second pair. The result is 5 in all groups except 5357. The difference between 57 and 53 is 4, not 5.

- *outside or inside*

1.   3004   4005   5004   6007

The inside two numbers are zero. The outside two numbers are consecutive ascending. 5004 is different because the outside two numbers are consecutive descending.

2.   5245   7687   9469   3453

The first and last numbers are the same and odd. The inside numbers are two numbers apart and even consecutive. 3453 is different because the inside numbers are only one number apart.

   These are suggestions for specific patterns. Combinations of several patterns may occur in any number group question. Try not to spend too much time analyzing the numbers. You only have 7 minutes to complete 20 question, that leaves about 21 seconds to answer each question.

Identifying Different Number Groups Practice Exercise

Directions: Circle the number group that is different.

1.	101	202	301	404
2.	1111	5555	9996	6666
3.	7654	9876	5431	4321
4.	4224	8448	1001	2112
5.	0816	1622	2432	3846
6.	9569	7347	3553	5125
7.	222	333	777	999
8.	2543	4523	3254	5438
9.	3210	7634	5321	9543
10.	3510	7918	5714	7816

Answers

1. **301**   The first and last numbers are the same with zero in the middle. 301 is different because the first and last numbers are not the same.

2. **9996**   All numbers are the same in each sequence. Instead of 9996, we would expect 9999 for a number with a similar pattern.

3. **5431**   All numbers are descending and consecutive. If 5431 had been 5432 it would have followed the pattern.

4. **1001**   The outside numbers are twice the inside number. 1 times 2 does not equal 0. 1001 is also the only odd number in the group.

5. **1622**   There is a common difference of 8 between the first pair of numbers and the last pair of numbers.
   (a) 0816   8 + 8 = 16   (b) 1624   16 + 8 = 24, not 22.

6. **3553**   The outside numbers are repeating and the inside digits are consecutive. The second number is 4 less than the first number. 55 is not consecutive, and 5 is not 4 less than 3.

7. **222**   All numbers are repeats. The only even repeating number is 222.

8. **5438**   All numbers have the digits 2, 3, 4, 5. The number 5438 does not have a 2.

9. **7634**   The first digit is odd. The last three digits are consecutive descending. The last three digits of 7634 are not consecutive.

10. **7816**   The first number is 2 less than the 2nd number. The last two numbers are twice the second number. 7816 is different because 7 is not 2 less than 8.

NUMBER GROUPS SAMPLE ANSWER SHEET

1 Ⓐ Ⓑ Ⓒ Ⓓ   6 Ⓐ Ⓑ Ⓒ Ⓓ   11 Ⓐ Ⓑ Ⓒ Ⓓ   16 Ⓐ Ⓑ Ⓒ Ⓓ

2 Ⓐ Ⓑ Ⓒ Ⓓ   7 Ⓐ Ⓑ Ⓒ Ⓓ   12 Ⓐ Ⓑ Ⓒ Ⓓ   17 Ⓐ Ⓑ Ⓒ Ⓓ

3 Ⓐ Ⓑ Ⓒ Ⓓ   8 Ⓐ Ⓑ Ⓒ Ⓓ   13 Ⓐ Ⓑ Ⓒ Ⓓ   18 Ⓐ Ⓑ Ⓒ Ⓓ

4 Ⓐ Ⓑ Ⓒ Ⓓ   9 Ⓐ Ⓑ Ⓒ Ⓓ   14 Ⓐ Ⓑ Ⓒ Ⓓ   19 Ⓐ Ⓑ Ⓒ Ⓓ

5 Ⓐ Ⓑ Ⓒ Ⓓ   10 Ⓐ Ⓑ Ⓒ Ⓓ   15 Ⓐ Ⓑ Ⓒ Ⓓ   20 Ⓐ Ⓑ Ⓒ Ⓓ

NUMBER GROUPS SAMPLE ANSWER
SHEET

NUMBER GROUPS PRACTICE TEST

Time: 7 Minutes. 20 Questions.

This test measures the ability to see how groups of numbers are alike and different.

Directions: *Each problem has four groups of numbers; three of the number groups have something in common. Darken the choice on your sample answer sheet which corresponds to the one group that is different from the other three.*

1.	(A) 4512	(B) 9514	(C) 5611	(D) 8715
2.	(A) 2929	(B) 5757	(C) 3838	(D) 1313
3.	(A) 1924	(B) 9590	(C) 5055	(D) 7277
4.	(A) 6453	(B) 5508	(C) 9162	(D) 7327
5.	(A) 3032	(B) 8086	(C) 5054	(D) 7076
6.	(A) 9867	(B) 5432	(C) 4321	(D) 7654
7.	(A) 1237	(B) 1437	(C) 1537	(D) 1637
8.	(A) 2244	(B) 8899	(C) 4466	(D) 5577
9.	(A) 9281	(B) 6545	(C) 7436	(D) 4918
10.	(A) 1582	(B) 1836	(C) 2173	(D) 3557
11.	(A) 5556	(B) 7879	(C) 8382	(D) 6263
12.	(A) 7853	(B) 7964	(C) 7642	(D) 7743
13.	(A) 9036	(B) 6024	(C) 3012	(D) 5030
14.	(A) 2244	(B) 3255	(C) 1277	(D) 4266
15.	(A) 6142	(B) 2468	(C) 4268	(D) 8642
16.	(A) 3355	(B) 7755	(C) 1133	(D) 5544
17.	(A) 9088	(B) 7072	(C) 8280	(D) 6462
18.	(A) 5525	(B) 8353	(C) 9565	(D) 6133
19.	(A) 9228	(B) 7227	(C) 5225	(D) 6226
20.	(A) 3263	(B) 4181	(C) 3354	(D) 1436

Explanatory Answers

1. **(A)** The first number plus the second number is equal to the last pair of numbers. 4512 is different because 4 + 5 does not equal the last number pair 12.

2. **(C)** All numbers are repeating pairs. 3838 is different because it is even.

3. **(B)** The first pair of numbers plus 5 is equal to the 2nd pair of numbers. 9590 is different because 95 plus 5 does not equal 90.

4. **(D)** The third plus the fourth number is equal to 8. 7327 is different because the third number 2 added to the fourth number 7 does not equal 8.

5. **(B)** The fourth number is one less than the third number. 8086 is different because 8 - 1 does not equal 6.

6. **(A)** All the number groups are in descending consecutive order. 9867 is not in order.

7. **(C)** All the numbers end in 37. The first pair of numbers are all even. 1537 has an odd first pair of numbers.

8. **(B)** The first pair plus 22 is the second pair. 88 plus 22 does not equal 99.

9. **(D)** The sum of the first and second number is 11. 4918 is different because 4 plus 9 equals 13 not 11.

10. **(A)** The first pair is equal to the third number times the fourth number. 1582 is different because 8 times 2 does not equal 15.

11. **(C)** The first pair plus 1 equals the second pair. 83 plus 1 does not equal 82.

12. **(B)** All the numbers begin with 7. The third number plus the fourth equals the second number. In 7964, 6 plus 4 does not equal 9.

13. **(D)** The first number times 4 is equal to the last pair of numbers. In the number 5030, 5 x 4 is not 30.

14. **(C)** The first number plus the second number equals the third number. In 1277, 1 plus 2 does not equal 7.

15. **(A)** All numbers are arrangements of 2, 4, 6, 8. The number 6142 does not have an 8.

16. **(D)** All numbers are repeating pairs of odd numbers. 5544 has an even pair.

17. **(B)** The first pair minus the second pair equals to 2. 70 minus 2 does not equal 72.

18. **(D)** The first pair minus the second pair is thirty. 61 minus 33 does not equal 30.

19. **(A)** 9228 is different because 9 and 8 are not the same.

20. **(C)** The first number plus the second number equals 5. 3354 is different because 3 plus 3 is not equal to 5.

PART V

Preparing for the

Spelling Section

Business Words List

This is a list from which you can begin to study for the spelling section of the BTAB. It consists of words that are commonly misspelled in business correspondence. Start with one letter group then continue until you have reviewed all the words. Do not memorize all the words in the list, but review the following section on spelling rules. Master the rules then memorize those that are exceptions.

Read through the list and make a list of the words whose meaning or spelling you are uncertain. Make this a practice list for a friend or peer to quiz you as you are studying.

A

abandonment	administration	appraisal
abatement	advances	approach
abdicate	advertisement	appropriation
aberration	advisability	approval
abetted	advise	arbitrator
abjuring	affects	arduous
abrogate	affectionate	argument
absence	affidavit	arguing
absolutely	affirmative	arrears
accept	agency	arrival
acceptance	aggravate	articles
accidentally	agriculture	askew
accolade	allotment	assessable
accommodate	allowance	assignment
accompany	all right	assimilate
accomplish	alphabetic	assistance
accountant	altercation	associate
accrual	altruism	assuage
accumulate	amateur	assumable
accurate	ameliorate	assured
accustomed	analogous	assurance
achievement	analysis	astute
acknowledgment	analyze	attached
acquainted	anniversary	attorney
acquire	announcement	attempt
acquisition	anthracite	attendance
acquitted	anticipating	attractive
actually	anxiety	auditor
additionally	apology	auspicious
address	apparatus	authority
abjudicate	appearance	available
acquiesce	appease	avarice
adjustable	applicant	aviation

B

badger
baggage
balance
bankruptcy
banquet
barrel
barter
basically
becoming
beginning
believe
beneficiary
benefited
benign
benevolent
biased
bibulous
bituminous
blithe
bolster
bookkeeping
borrower
bounteous
brevity
brief
broadcast
brokerage
boundary
budget
bulletin
bureau
business

C

calamity
calculator
calendar
camouflage
campaign
canceled
candidate
capacity
capitalization
carbon
caricature
carrier
cartage
carton
category
caustic
certificate
chattel
chaperone
characteristic
chief
circular
circuit
circumstance
civilization
clearance
clandestine
coincidence
collapsible
collateral
collision
colloquial
column
combination
combustible
commerce
commission
committee
commodity
community
companies
comparative
comparison
compatible
compel
compensation
competent
competition

complaint
complimentary
compunction
conceivable
conception
concession
concomitant
conciliate
condemn
confidential
conference
confirmation
congestion
connotation
conscientious
conscious
consequence
considerable
consignee
conspicuous
consolidated
constitution
construction
consumer
container
contemplating
contemporary
contingent
control
contumacious
convenience
conveyance
cooperate
corporation
correspondence
corroborate
corrugated
counterfeit
coupon
courteous
credentials
creditor
credulous
criticize
curiosity
currency
customer
cylinder

D

daunt
debauch
debilitate
decision
defendant
deferred
deficit
definite
defray
deleterious
delightfully
demonstration
depreciation
descended
description
desperate
destination
deteriorate
determination
deterrent
detonation
detriment
develop
dictionary
director
disappear
disappoint
disastrous
disbursements
discernible
discipline
discontinued
discrepancy
discursive
discuss
disgusted
disparage
dispatch
dissatisfaction
dissolution
distinction
distinguish
distributor
diversify
dividend
document
dominant
dominion

doubt
duplicate
durable
duration

E

earliest
earnest
easier
easement
ebullient
economic
efficiency
effusion
elevator
egalitarian
eighth
eligible
embarrassment
emergency
employee
encouraging
enormous
enterprise
envelope
environment
equally
equipped
especially
estimate
essentially
eventually
evidence
exaggerate
examination
exasperate
exceedingly
excellent
except
exchange
executive
exemplary
exhibition
existence
expedite
explanation
extension

F
facilitate
fallacy
fascinating
fastidious
fatal
favorably
February
fervent
fervor
fictitious
fiduciary
financier
florescence
flounderforay
forbearance
forbidden
foreclosure
forehead
forfeit
formally
formative
formerly
formula
fortuitous
forty
fracas
franchise
frequent
fundamental
furniture
furlough
furtive
futile

G
generally
genuine
germane
gerontology
glamourous
glimpse
glorious
grabbed
gracious
graduating
government
grammar
gross

guile
gullible
gymnasium

H
handkerchief
happiness
harmonious
hastily
hazard
heavily
height
heritage
heuristic
hindrance
honorarium
hoping
hosiery
humorous
hypocrisy
hypocritical
hypothesize

I
ignorance
illegible
illuminate
imagination
immediately
immense
imminent
immiscible
immoderate
immutable
impermeable
impracticable
impregnable
inadvertent
inasmuch
inauspicious
incidentally
incomparable
incongruous
inconsequential
inconsistent
inconvenience
inconvertible
inconspicuous

incorporated
incredible
increment
incriminating
inculcate
indefatigable
indelible
indolence
indemnity
indispensable
inducement
industrial
inevitable
ineffable
inferred
inflation
infringement
initiate
innocuous
inquiry
insipid
insolvency
inspection
instance
instigate
institution
instructor
insufficient
insurance
intangible
integrity
intelligence
intermittent
interrogate
interpretation
interrupt
intrepid
inventory
investigate
invoice
involved
irascible
itemized
itinerary
its

J
jealous
jeopardize
jobber
jocular
journal
judgment
juxtapose

K
keenness
knowledge

L
laboratory
ladies
laudable
lauded
latter
leased
ledger
legitimate
leisure
lengthen
lethargic
liabilities
library
license
likable or likeable
liquidation
literature
locator
loneliness
lucrative
luscious
luxury

M
machinery
magazine
maintenance
management
maneuver
manila
manufacturer
margin
marred

material
matriculate
maturity
meander
mechanical
medicine
mellifluous
memorandum
merchandise
mercantile
merge
meridian
meritorious
middleman
millennium
mimeograph
minimum
miniature
miscellaneous
misrepresent
misspelled
mitigate
moistener
monopoly
monotonous
monumental
mortgage
movie
mucilage
mundane
municipal
muscle
mutual
mystifying

N
necessary
niece
ninth
nondescript
nonpartisan
notably
notary
noticeable
notwithstanding
nowadays

nucleus
nullify
numeral
numerator
nutritious
nylon

O
obedience
obliging
obliterate
oblivious
obscure
observation
obsolete
obstacle
obtrude
occasionally
occurred
offense
official
omission
oneself
operations
oppresion
opportunity
optimism
option
orchestra
ordinance
organization
outrageous
overdraw
overhead
oxygen

P
pamphlet
palatable
paradise
parallel
parenthesis
parliament
particularly
partition

pavilion
paternalism
peaceable
peculiarities
pecuniary
percent
perforation
performance
permanent
permissible
peripheral
perpendicular
perseverance
personal
personnel
persuade
perspiration
perusal
petition
petroleum
phantom
phenomenal
philosopher
photostat
physical
physician
plaintiff
plausible
pleasant
policy
practically
precedence
precise
preface
preference
prejudice
preparation
prescription
presence
presidency
prestige
pretentious
primitive
principal
principle
privilege
probably

problematic
procedure
proceed
process
procrastinate
prodigious
professional
profligate
prominence
promissory
pronunciation
prospectus
proselytize
protested
protuberance
psychology
publicity
pursuit

Q
qualification
quantity
questionnaire
quiescence
quietus
quotation

R
rambunctious
ramification
readjustment
really
reasonable
rebate
receipt
recognize
reconcilable
recommend
reconstruction
reference
regardless
register
regimen
regretfully
reimburse

reinforcement
relations
relieve
remedied
remittance
removal
repercussion
repertoire
replenish
representative
requisition
rescind
resign
respectfully
respectively
responsible
responsibility
resuscitate
restaurant
reticence
revere
revitalize
rhythm
ridiculous
rural

S

sacrifice
sagacious
salary
salutation
sanctimonious
sanitary
satisfactory
scarcely
schedule
schismatic
scissors
scrupulour
scrutinize
secretarial
security
seize
senate
seniority
separate
servile
several

significance
similar
simultaneous
sincerely
skeptical
sociable
society
solemn
solvent
sometimes
sophisticated
sophomore
source
southern
souvenir
specialize
specify
spectacular
speculate
squallid
stagnant
stanza
statement
stationary
stationery
statistics
stoic
straightened
strenuous
strictly
stringent
sublet
subsidize
substantial
substitute
subtle
successful
sufficient
suggestion
supercilious
summary
superfluous
superintendent
surplus
susceptible
sychophant
syndicate
systematize

T

tangible
tariff
tautology
tedium
tendency
testimonials
thorough
tickler
titillation
titillated
together
transferring
tranquility
transferred
transparent
transcend
treasurer
tremendous
trepidation
triplicate
truly
Tuesday
turnover
turpitude
typewriter
typical
typographical

U

unanimous
unbelievable
undermine
undulant
unfortunately
university
unmistakable
unnecessary
unprecedented
urgent
useful
utilities
utilize

V

vacancies
vacillate
vacuum
vagrant
valid
varies
vehement
verbose
verification
vicinity
vilify
virtually
virulent
virtuoso
visible
voices
volatile
volume
voluminous
voracity
voucher
vulnerable

W

waive
warrant
Wednesday
whatever
wholesale
wholly
women

Spelling Rules

Here are a few of the most common spelling rules for you to master. Most of the rules in spelling can be learned if you are familiar with the root of the word. Many spelling rules concern silent endings, double consonants, adding a prefix or suffix, and past tense plurals. These rules are helpful to learn so that you can spell without having to look up every word in the dictionary.

The ie rule

The first rule that comes to mind when you think of spelling is " i before e except after c". There's another part to the rhyme that goes, " or when sounded like ay, as in neighbor or weigh".

Exceptions: Neither, leisure, foreigner, seized, weird, heights.

Several examples in your word list follow the *ie* rule.

brief	convenience	handkerchief	hosiery	receipt
carrier	eighth	inconvenience	movie	unbelievable

These are examples in your word list that are exceptions to the *ie* rule.

conscientious	efficiency	reimburse
financier	society	height
seize	reinforcement	counterfeit
forfeit	leisure	

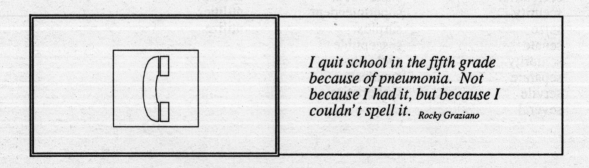

I quit school in the fifth grade because of pneumonia. Not because I had it, but because I couldn't spell it. Rocky Graziano

92

Spelling Exercise One

<u>Directions</u>: *Circle the word spelled correctly in the parentheses using the ie rule.*

1.   The customer signed the (receipt, reciept) for the printer.

2.   It was a great (relief, releif) to get away from the office.

3.   Arlan gave a loud (shriek, shreik) and ran into the forest.

4.   The soldiers refused to (yeild, yield) their positions.

5.   She was a perfect (fiend, feind) in her behavior.

6.   Her (acheivement, achievement) was remarkable for her age.

7.   Once you have lost your reputation, it is difficult to (retreive, retrieve) it.

8.   Good (freinds, friends) are hard to find.

9.   The slain leader was carried to the (beir, bier).

10.   He was (chief, cheif) of the local police department.

11.   We were (receiveing, receiving) contributions all day .

12.   It is difficult to (deceive, decieve) your parents all the time.

13.   Strenuous efforts are required to (achieve, acheive) an Olympic gold medal.

14.   Astronomers can now (percieve, perceive) stars that are quite small.

15.   Our (neighbors, nieghbors) to the south were angry at our behavior.

16.   Careless training may lead to such (mischievious, mischievous) behavior in childhood.

17.   The last (frontier, fronteir) is now in space.

18.   Although the (ceiling, cieling) was low, he bought the house.

19.   We were spending our afternoon in (leisure, liesure).

20.   Napolean wanted to (sieze, seize) more nations for his conquest.

Answers to Exercise One

1. receipt	6. achievement	11. receiving	16. mischievous
2. relief	7. retrieve	12. deceive	17. frontier
3. shriek	8. friends	13. achieve	18. ceiling
4. yield	9. bier*	14. perceive	19. leisure
5. fiend	10. chief	15. neighbors	20. seize

* You may have never heard of this word. It is the place where a corpse is laid. The pronunciation is similar to pier. Nevertheless, if you had followed the rule, you would have correctly spelled this word.

Rules for words ending in y:

- If a word ends in *y* preceded by a vowel, keep the *y* when adding a suffix.

  <u>Examples</u>: day, days; attorney, attorneys

- If a word ends in *y* preceded by a consonant, change the *y* to *i* before adding a suffix.

  <u>Examples</u>: try, tries, tried; lady, ladies

- *Exceptions*: To avoid double i, retain the y before ing and ish.

  <u>Examples</u>: fly, flying; baby, babyish; mystify, mystifying

Rules about silent e:

° • Silent e at the end of a word is usually dropped before a suffix beginning with a vowel.

> Examples: dine + ing = dining
>   locate + ion = location
>   use + able = usable
>   offense + ive = offensive

Exceptions: Words ending in *ce* and *ge* retain e before the suffix *able* and *ous* in order to retain their soft sounds.

> Examples: peaceable + able = peaceable
>   courage + ous = courageous

• Silent *e* is usually kept before a suffix beginning with a consonant.

> Examples: care + less = careless
>   immediate + ly = immediately
>   late + ly = lately
>   one + ness = oneness
>   game + ster = gamester

• Some exceptions must simply be memorized. Some exceptions to the silent *e* rule are: truly, duly, awful, argument, wholly, ninth, mileage, dyeing, acreage, canoeing.

Suggestion: Spelling rules only have a few exceptions. When in doubt use the rule!

Spelling Exercise Two

<u>*Directions*</u>: *Examples of words ending in silent e from the word list are included below. Write the root word for each and identify the suffix which causes you to drop the e.*

WORD	ROOT WORD	SUFFIX
anticipating	——————	——————
contemplating	——————	——————
incriminating	——————	——————
noticeable	——————	——————
likeable	——————	——————
assumable	——————	——————
administration	——————	——————
appropriation	——————	——————
compensation	——————	——————
corporation	——————	——————
demonstration	——————	——————
depreciation	——————	——————
inflation	——————	——————
institution	——————	——————
liquidation	——————	——————
perforation	——————	——————
titillation	——————	——————

Answers to Exercise Two

WORD	ROOT WORD	SUFFIX
anticipating	anticipate	ing
contemplating	contemplate	ing
incriminating	incriminate	ing
noticeable	notice	able
likeable	like	able
assumable	assume	able
administration	administrate	ion
appropriation	appropriate	ion
compensation	compensate	ion
corporation	corporate	ion
demonstration	demonstrate	ion
depreciation	depreciate	ion
inflation	inflate	ion
institution	institute	ion
liquidation	liquidate	ion
perforation	perforate	ion
pronunciation	pronunciate	ion
titillation	titillate	ion

Rules for words ending in a single consonant preceded by a single vowel

- A word of one syllable that ends in a single consonant preceded by a single vowel doubles the final consonant before a suffix beginning with a vowel or *y*.

    Examples: hit, hitting; drop, dropped; big, biggest; mud, muddy; but: help, helping because help ends in two consonants; need, needing, needy does not double the because the final consonant (d) is preceded by two vowels.

- A word of more than one syllable that accents the last syllable and that ends in a single consonant preceded by a single vowel doubles the final consonant when adding a suffix beginning with a vowel.

    Examples: begin, beginner; admit, admitted; but: enter, entered because the accent is not on the last syllable.

Spelling Exercise Three

Directions: *Identify the root word and corresponding rule.*

WORD	ROOT	RULE
acquitted	———————	———————
baggage	———————	———————
remittance	———————	———————
transferred	———————	———————

Answers to Exercise Three

WORD	ROOT	RULE
acquitted	acquit	two syllable word double the *t* because there is an *i* before the *t* and you are adding a vowel suffix *ed*
baggage	bag	one syllable word double the *g* before the suffix age which begins with a vowel
remittance	remit	two syllable word double the *t* because there is an *i* before the *t* and you are adding a vowel suffix ance
transfer	transferred	two syllable word double the *r* because there is an *e* before the *r* and you are adding a vowel suffix *ed*

Words ending in *er*

- A word ending in *er* double the *r* in the past tense if the word is accented on the last syllable.

  Example: prefer, preferred; transfer, transferred

- A word ending in *er* does not double the *r* in the past tense if the accent falls before the last syllable.

  Examples: answer, answered; offer, offered; differ, differed

Spelling Exercise Four

Directions: Correctly spell the past tense for each of these words from the list.

1. barter _____   4. infer _____

2. consider _____   5. register _____

3. defer _____   6. transfer _____

Answers to Exercise Four

1. bartered   3. deferred   5. registered
2. considered   4. inferred   6. transferred

Additional rules to remember

1. When *full* is added to the end of a noun, the final l is dropped.

   <u>Examples:</u>   cheerful, cupful, hopeful

2. All words beginning with *over* are one word.

   <u>Examples:</u>   overcast, overcharge, overhear, overeat, overcome

3. All words with the prefix *self* are hyphenated.

   <u>Examples:</u>   self-control, self-defense, self-evident, self-employed, self-esteem

4. The letter *q* is always followed by *u*.

   <u>Examples:</u>   qualification, quantity, questionnaire, quotation

5. Numbers from twenty-one to ninety-nine are hyphenated.

6. Per cent is never hyphenated. It may be written as one word (percent) or as two words (per cent).

7. Welcome is one word with one l.

8. All right is always two words.

9. Already means prior to some specified time. All ready means completely ready.

   <u>Example:</u>   By the time I was all ready to go to the play, the tickets were already sold out.

10. Altogether means entirely.
    All together means in sum or collectively.

    <u>Example:</u>   There are altogether too many people to seat in this room when we are all together.

SPELLING TEST I

Since the BTAB requires that you select the correct spelling from four sentence fragments, use this practice exercise to recognize misspelled words.

Directions: Some of the words below are correctly spelled and some are not. Where the spelling is WRONG, write the correct spelling in the space following the word. Do nothing when a word is spelled correctly.

1. procrastinate
2. goverment
3. asumable
4. accidant
5. deside
6. accept
7. nullify
8. already
9. committe
10. bussiness
11. minute
12. regretfuly
13. realy
14. consideration
15. tranquillity
16. invoise
17. assure
18. foriegn
19. sophisticated
20. responsability

21. reconcileable _____

22. application _____

23. develope _____

24. issue _____

25. receive _____

26. descended _____

27. agreement _____

28. incomparable _____

29. arrangement _____

30. experiance _____

31. mellifloous _____

32. charactor _____

33. organization _____

34. aswuage _____

35. atheletic _____

36. practical _____

37. photograph _____

38. instrament _____

39. decision _____

40. proposel _____

Answers to Spelling Test I

2. government

3. assumable

4. accident

5. decide

9. committee

10. business

12. regretfully

13. really

15. tranquility

16. invoice

18. foreign

20. responsibility

21. reconcilable

23. develop

30. experience

31. mellifluous

32. character

34. assuage

35. athletic

38. instrument

40. proposal

All other words have been spelled correctly.

Suggestions for Study

Make a list of your misspelled problem words for another test or spelling bee with other test takers or friends.

If you miss a word immediately put a large X on the letter that you missed. Then rewrite the word correctly with a large correct letter. This should help you to visualize the incorrect spelling as well as the correct spelling when you are asked to spell the word again.

Example: Suppose you spelled *tenacious* as *tinacious*.

      tXnacious   Put a large X on the incorrect i.

      tEnacious   Rewrite tenacious with a large E where the misspelling occurred.

SPELLING TEST II

Here is a list of words to study for a practice spelling exam.

<u>Directions</u>: *Make a sentence with each word so that you can remember its spelling and usage.*

extravagant   _____

photogenic   _____

facetious   _____

relinquish   _____

heterogeneous   _____

tenacious   _____

malicious   _____

diagnostic   _____

lucrative   _____

coincidence   _____

obnoxious   _____

voice   _____

unbelievable   _____

arbitrary   _____

SPELLING SAMPLE ANSWER SHEET

1 Ⓐ Ⓑ Ⓒ Ⓓ   3 Ⓐ Ⓑ Ⓒ Ⓓ   5 Ⓐ Ⓑ Ⓒ Ⓓ   7 Ⓐ Ⓑ Ⓒ Ⓓ   9 Ⓐ Ⓑ Ⓒ Ⓓ

2 Ⓐ Ⓑ Ⓒ Ⓓ   4 Ⓐ Ⓑ Ⓒ Ⓓ   6 Ⓐ Ⓑ Ⓒ Ⓓ   8 Ⓐ Ⓑ Ⓒ Ⓓ   10 Ⓐ Ⓑ Ⓒ Ⓓ

SPELLING PRACTICE TEST

Time: 5 Minutes. 10 Questions.

This test measures your ability to spell words correctly.

Directions: *For each question a test assistant will pronounce a word to be spelled and then use it in a sentence. Mark the letter series from the answer choices that is contained in the correct spelling of the word. If you do not have someone to read the words, record them yourself and play them back when you begin the test.*

To the Test Assistant: *Turn to page 109 for the spelling list and corresponding sentences.*

1. The word you have just spelled contains which of the following series of letters?
    (A) nock   (B) shou   (C) noxi   (D) noex

2. The word you have just spelled contains which of the following series of letters?
    (A) foto   (B) phot   (C) gini   (D) nick

3. The word you have just spelled contains which of the following series of letters?
    (A) ooce   (B) oece   (C) ouce   (D) oice

4. The word you have just spelled contains which of the following series of letters?
    (A) gine   (B) ginu   (C) gino   (D) gene

5. The word you have just spelled contains which of the following series of letters?
    (A) aveg   (B) avag   (C) vage   (D) egen

6. The word you have just spelled contains which of the following series of letters?
    (A) tina   (B) sous   (C) tena   (D) hous

7. The word you have just spelled contains which of the following series of letters?
    (A) kwis   (B) nkis   (C) lenq   (D) quis

8. The word you have just spelled contains which of the following series of letters?
    (A) mali   (B) meli   (C) male   (D) alis

9. The word you have just spelled contains which of the following series of letters?
    (A) anos   (B) agno   (C) egno   (D) ieno

10. The word you have just spelled contains which of the following series of letters?
    (A) evab   (B) eiva   (C) evib   (D) vabe

Practice Word Search

<u>*Directions*</u>: *Practice recognizing the correct spelling for each word by solving this Word Search puzzle that contains ten words from the word list in the beginning of this section. Answers on page 109.*

```
U P F G R E L I N Q U I S H H
P N R G E C M N B Y R W Q D E
P P B C M I E E E P Q W E I T
H E T E R O G E N E O U S A R
O T J O L V D I A G N O S G O
T H R B E I L I N Q U I S N G
O J E N H E E T E R E G E O E
G K T O E N A V C I O U S S N
E L E X T R A V A G A N T T O
N L V I C O E M A B L T E I U
I S U O I C A N E T L E C C S
C O C U F U F O T M N E P Y E
Q P T S U O I C I L A M R W C
```

To the Test Assistant.

Directions: Read each word and the sentence using that word. Pause 17 seconds before reading the next word to allow the test taker to answer the questions. Do not repeat any word or sentence.

1. *obnoxious* -- The smell from the river is obnoxious at night.
2. *photogenic* -- The doctor had a photogenic memory.
3. *voice* -- We live in a country that allows us to voice our opinion.
4. *heterogeneous* -- The heterogeneous art collection was a great representation of that era.
5. *extravagant* -- They were so extravagant that they went into debt.
6. *tenacious* -- The dog has a tenacious hold on the stick.
7. *relinquish* -- The dog would not relinquish the shoe.
8. *malicious* -- They spread malicious rumors to hurt his reelection campaign.
9. *diagnostic* -- The diagnostic test revealed that I had diabetes.
10. *unbelievable* -- It is unbelievable how much you can forget after leaving high school.

Answers to Spelling Practice Test

1. (C)	3. (D)	5. (B)	7. (D)	9. (B)
2. (B)	4. (D)	6. (C)	8. (A)	10. (A)

Answers to Practice Word Search

```
U           R E L I N Q U I S H
   N           C               D
P     B        I               I
H  E  T  E R   O G E N E O U S  A
O     O  R  L  V               G
T     B  L  I                  N
O     N     E                  O
G     O        V               S
E     E X T R A V A G A N T     T
N     I          B    L        I
I  S  U  I C A N E T  L        C
C     O              E
   U  S  U O I C I L A M
```

PART VI

Model BTAB Tests

MODEL TEST ONE ANSWER SHEET

COMPUTATIONAL FACILITY

1 Ⓐ Ⓑ Ⓒ Ⓓ	5 Ⓐ Ⓑ Ⓒ Ⓓ	9 Ⓐ Ⓑ Ⓒ Ⓓ	13 Ⓐ Ⓑ Ⓒ Ⓓ	17 Ⓐ Ⓑ Ⓒ Ⓓ
2 Ⓐ Ⓑ Ⓒ Ⓓ	6 Ⓐ Ⓑ Ⓒ Ⓓ	10 Ⓐ Ⓑ Ⓒ Ⓓ	14 Ⓐ Ⓑ Ⓒ Ⓓ	18 Ⓐ Ⓑ Ⓒ Ⓓ
3 Ⓐ Ⓑ Ⓒ Ⓓ	7 Ⓐ Ⓑ Ⓒ Ⓓ	11 Ⓐ Ⓑ Ⓒ Ⓓ	15 Ⓐ Ⓑ Ⓒ Ⓓ	19 Ⓐ Ⓑ Ⓒ Ⓓ
4 Ⓐ Ⓑ Ⓒ Ⓓ	8 Ⓐ Ⓑ Ⓒ Ⓓ	12 Ⓐ Ⓑ Ⓒ Ⓓ	16 Ⓐ Ⓑ Ⓒ Ⓓ	20 Ⓐ Ⓑ Ⓒ Ⓓ

FOLLOWING DIRECTIONS

1 Ⓐ Ⓑ Ⓒ Ⓓ	6 Ⓐ Ⓑ Ⓒ Ⓓ	11 Ⓐ Ⓑ Ⓒ Ⓓ
2 Ⓐ Ⓑ Ⓒ Ⓓ	7 Ⓐ Ⓑ Ⓒ Ⓓ	12 Ⓐ Ⓑ Ⓒ Ⓓ
3 Ⓐ Ⓑ Ⓒ Ⓓ	8 Ⓐ Ⓑ Ⓒ Ⓓ	13 Ⓐ Ⓑ Ⓒ Ⓓ
4 Ⓐ Ⓑ Ⓒ Ⓓ	9 Ⓐ Ⓑ Ⓒ Ⓓ	14 Ⓐ Ⓑ Ⓒ Ⓓ
5 Ⓐ Ⓑ Ⓒ Ⓓ	10 Ⓐ Ⓑ Ⓒ Ⓓ	15 Ⓐ Ⓑ Ⓒ Ⓓ

NUMBER GROUPS

1 Ⓐ Ⓑ Ⓒ Ⓓ	5 Ⓐ Ⓑ Ⓒ Ⓓ	9 Ⓐ Ⓑ Ⓒ Ⓓ	13 Ⓐ Ⓑ Ⓒ Ⓓ	17 Ⓐ Ⓑ Ⓒ Ⓓ
2 Ⓐ Ⓑ Ⓒ Ⓓ	6 Ⓐ Ⓑ Ⓒ Ⓓ	10 Ⓐ Ⓑ Ⓒ Ⓓ	14 Ⓐ Ⓑ Ⓒ Ⓓ	18 Ⓐ Ⓑ Ⓒ Ⓓ
3 Ⓐ Ⓑ Ⓒ Ⓓ	7 Ⓐ Ⓑ Ⓒ Ⓓ	11 Ⓐ Ⓑ Ⓒ Ⓓ	15 Ⓐ Ⓑ Ⓒ Ⓓ	19 Ⓐ Ⓑ Ⓒ Ⓓ
4 Ⓐ Ⓑ Ⓒ Ⓓ	8 Ⓐ Ⓑ Ⓒ Ⓓ	12 Ⓐ Ⓑ Ⓒ Ⓓ	16 Ⓐ Ⓑ Ⓒ Ⓓ	20 Ⓐ Ⓑ Ⓒ Ⓓ

SPELLING

1 Ⓐ Ⓑ Ⓒ Ⓓ	7 Ⓐ Ⓑ Ⓒ Ⓓ	13 Ⓐ Ⓑ Ⓒ Ⓓ	19 Ⓐ Ⓑ Ⓒ Ⓓ	25 Ⓐ Ⓑ Ⓒ Ⓓ
2 Ⓐ Ⓑ Ⓒ Ⓓ	8 Ⓐ Ⓑ Ⓒ Ⓓ	14 Ⓐ Ⓑ Ⓒ Ⓓ	20 Ⓐ Ⓑ Ⓒ Ⓓ	26 Ⓐ Ⓑ Ⓒ Ⓓ
3 Ⓐ Ⓑ Ⓒ Ⓓ	9 Ⓐ Ⓑ Ⓒ Ⓓ	15 Ⓐ Ⓑ Ⓒ Ⓓ	21 Ⓐ Ⓑ Ⓒ Ⓓ	27 Ⓐ Ⓑ Ⓒ Ⓓ
4 Ⓐ Ⓑ Ⓒ Ⓓ	10 Ⓐ Ⓑ Ⓒ Ⓓ	16 Ⓐ Ⓑ Ⓒ Ⓓ	22 Ⓐ Ⓑ Ⓒ Ⓓ	28 Ⓐ Ⓑ Ⓒ Ⓓ
5 Ⓐ Ⓑ Ⓒ Ⓓ	11 Ⓐ Ⓑ Ⓒ Ⓓ	17 Ⓐ Ⓑ Ⓒ Ⓓ	23 Ⓐ Ⓑ Ⓒ Ⓓ	29 Ⓐ Ⓑ Ⓒ Ⓓ
6 Ⓐ Ⓑ Ⓒ Ⓓ	12 Ⓐ Ⓑ Ⓒ Ⓓ	18 Ⓐ Ⓑ Ⓒ Ⓓ	24 Ⓐ Ⓑ Ⓒ Ⓓ	30 Ⓐ Ⓑ Ⓒ Ⓓ

Model Test One

COMPUTATIONAL FACILITY

Time: 9 Minutes. 20 Questions.

This test measures the ability to do arithmetic problems accurately.

Directions: *Solve each of the following mathematical operations. Mark your answers on the sample answer sheet.*

1. $2.217 + 0.759$
   - (A) 2.976
   - (B) 3.976
   - (C) 9.707
   - (D) 2.966

2. $4231 - 589$
   - (A) 5652
   - (B) 3641
   - (C) 3642
   - (D) 3652

3. $2\frac{2}{5} \div 8\frac{1}{3}$
   - (A) 20
   - (B) 1/20
   - (C) 3/10
   - (D) 36/125

4. $11 - 1\frac{2}{3}$
   - (A) 9 1/3
   - (B) 10 1/3
   - (C) 9 2/3
   - (D) 10 2/3

5. $9324 \div 36$
   - (A) 249
   - (B) 259
   - (C) 254
   - (D) 244

6. 45% of what is 54.9?
   - (A) 82
   - (B) 1.22
   - (C) 122
   - (D) 12.2

7. What percent of 365 is 116.8?

    (A) 32%
    (B) 3.13%
    (C) 320%
    (D) 31%

8. 87.23 x 4.6

    (A) 401.258
    (B) 40.1258
    (C) 401.244
    (D) 4.01258

9. $14\frac{2}{5} \times 8\frac{1}{3}$

    (A) 10 1/3
    (B) 12
    (C) 300
    (D) 120

10. $13\frac{2}{3} + 21\frac{1}{6}$

    (A) 35
    (B) 34 5/6
    (C) 34 3/18
    (D) 34 3/9

11. 146.27 - 85.88

    (A) 61.49
    (B) 60.49
    (C) 61.39
    (D) 60.39

12. 212,769 + 14,580

    (A) 227,329
    (B) 237,349
    (C) 226,349
    (D) 227,349

13. What is 60% of 84?

    (A) 5.04
    (B) 50.4
    (C) 504
    (D) None of the Above

14. $\frac{7}{24} - \frac{3}{16}$

    (A) 1/2
    (B) 4
    (C) 5/48
    (D) 4/8

15. 1.536 ÷ 16

(A) 9.6
(B) .104
(C) 9.567
(D) None of the Above

16. $\dfrac{9}{8} \times \dfrac{16}{27}$

(A) 3/2
(B) 1 1/2
(C) 2/3
(D) 48/267

17. 93 + 25 + 24 + 16 + 45

(A) 203
(B) 213
(C) 193
(D) 113

18. What is .4% of 125?

(A) .5
(B) 5
(C) 50
(D) .05

19. 245.6 + 87.344 + 13

(A) 89.813
(B) 898.13
(C) 345.944
(D) 349.44

20. 8392 × 61

(A) 510,812
(B) 511,812
(C) 511,813
(D) 511,912

FOLLOWING DIRECTIONS

Time: 10 Minutes. 15 Questions.

This test measures your ability to follow both written and oral instructions.

Directions: Use the table below to follow the written and oral directions. Mark your answers on the sample answer sheet.

To the Test Assistant: Turn to page 125 for the oral instructions. If you do not have someone to read the oral directions for you, record them yourself and play them back when you begin the exam.

	Column				
	1	2	3	4	5
Row 1	A	D	B	A	E
Row 2	B	B	A	B	E
Row 3	A	C	D	D	E
Row 4	D	B	B	D	D
Row 5	E	A	C	B	D

1. What letter is always to the left of C?

   (A) A   (B) B   (C) D   (D) E

2. Find the letter on Row 2 Column 4.

   (A) A   (B) B   (C) D   (D) E

3. Mark the letter that is always just above A.

   (A) B   (B) C   (C) D   (D) E

4. Which row has five different letters?

   (A) 1   (B) 2   (C) 3   (D) 5

5. Which column does not have the letter B twice?

   (A) 1   (B) 2   (C) 3   (D) 4

6. Count the letters in Column 5, what is the total?

   (A) 5   (B) 6   (C) 4   (D) 7

7. Which letter is first and last in the same row?

   (A) A   (B) B   (C) C   (D) D

8. Which letter occurs in two of the corners of the table?

   (A) A   (B) C   (C) D   (D) E

9. What is the total number of letters in the table?

   (A) 10   (B) 25   (C) 30   (D) 35

10. How many times does the letter B appear in the table?

    (A) 7   (B) 4   (C) 5   (D) 6

11. Find the row containing a four letter word and mark the correct response.

    (A) 1   (B) 2   (C) 3   (D) 4

12. Find the column containing only two different letters and mark the correct response.

    (A) 1   (B) 3   (C) 5   (D) 2

13. Locate the row that contains only two different letters and mark the correct response.

    (A) 1   (B) 2   (C) 3   (D) 4

14. If Row 5 was reversed, what letter would be just above the letter just above the letter to the right of the letter C?

    (A) A   (B) C   (C) D   (D) E

15. What letter is two spaces to the left of the letter that is just above the letter that is to the right of the next to the last letter in row 3?

    (A) A   (B) C   (C) D   (D) E

NUMBER GROUPS

Time: 7 Minutes. 20 Questions.

This is a test of your ability to see how groups of numbers are alike or different.

Directions: Each problem has four groups of numbers; three of the number groups have something in common. Darken the space on your sample answer sheet which corresponds to the one group that is different from the other three.

1.	(A) 6646	(B) 5575	(C) 4464	(D) 3353
2.	(A) 1159	(B) 1133	(C) 1172	(D) 1153
3.	(A) 5060	(B) 7080	(C) 1020	(D) 3050
4.	(A) 121224	(B) 9918	(C) 5510	(D) 141448
5.	(A) 477	(B) 253	(C) 586	(D) 364
6.	(A) 7890	(B) 5670	(C) 3460	(D) 1230
7.	(A) 6842	(B) 4268	(C) 5214	(D) 2684
8.	(A) 357	(B) 195	(C) 468	(D) 246
9.	(A) 634	(B) 847	(C) 425	(D) 214
10.	(A) 1234	(B) 7654	(C) 3456	(D) 5678
11.	(A) 3254	(B) 5492	(C) 6325	(D) 2548
12.	(A) 371	(B) 461	(C) 173	(D) 713
13.	(A) 456	(B) 345	(C) 223	(D) 567
14.	(A) 164	(B) 386	(C) 497	(D) 259
15.	(A) 284	(B) 757	(C) 531	(D) 953
16.	(A) 343	(B) 864	(C) 989	(D) 626
17.	(A) 5622	(B) 8933	(C) 4388	(D) 6755
18.	(A) 9402	(B) 9208	(C) 9204	(D) 9206
19.	(A) 2515	(B) 8575	(C) 6555	(D) 4555
20.	(A) 757	(B) 646	(C) 545	(D) 424

SPELLING

Time: 12 Minutes. 30 Questions.

This test measures your ability to spell words correctly.

Directions: *For each question a test assistant will pronounce a word to be spelled and then use it in a sentence. Mark the series of letters from the answer choices that is contained in the correct spelling of the word. If you do not have someone to read the words, record them yourself and play them back when you begin the test.*

To the Test Assistant: *Turn to pages 125-126 for the spelling list and corresponding sentences.*

1. The word you have just spelled contains which of the following series of letters?
   (A) lawd   (B) lard   (C) laud   (D) udid

2. The word you have just spelled contains which of the following series of letters?
   (A) assim   (B) asemm   (C) melat   (D) asimi

3. The word you have just spelled contains which of the following series of letters?
   (A) titel   (B) titte   (C) teion   (D) llati

4. The word you have just spelled contains which of the following series of letters?
   (A) consi   (B) conci   (C) lible   (D) llable

5. The word you have just spelled contains which of the following series of letters?
   (A) assua   (B) asaua   (C) asha   (D) aswag

6. The word you have just spelled contains which of the following series of letters?
   (A) cuss   (B) cous   (C) cuous   (D) picku

7. The word you have just spelled contains which of the following series of letters?
   (A) awsp   (B) shous   (C) ausp   (D) icous

8. The word you have just spelled contains which of the following series of letters?
   (A) vert   (B) virtu   (C) tualy   (D) tualie

9. The word you have just spelled contains which of the following series of letters?

    (A) scuw   (B) aske   (C) sque   (D)ascu

10. The word you have just spelled contains which of the following series of letters?

    (A) uitus   (B) utouis   (C) tious   (D)tous

11. The word you have just spelled contains which of the following series of letters?

    (A) rence   (B) rance   (C) burence   (D) tubur

12. The word you have just spelled contains which of the following series of letters?

    (A) terrog   (B) terog   (C) tarrog   (D) tarog

13. The word you have just spelled contains which of the following series of letters?

    (A) tentu   (B) ntous   (C) tinti   (D) tious

14. The word you have just spelled contains which of the following series of letters?

    (A) scend   (B) scind   (C) send   (D) ncend

15. The word you have just spelled contains which of the following series of letters?

    (A) natieng   (B) menat   (C) minat   (D) increm

16. The word you have just spelled contains which of the following series of letters?

    (A) mist   (B) fieng   (C) myst   (D) eing

17. The word you have just spelled contains which of the following series of letters?

    (A) eccem   (B) plery   (C) plory   (D) exem

18. The word you have just spelled contains which of the following series of letters?

    (A) imisc   (B) iscib   (C) sible   (D) mmic

19. The word you have just spelled contains which of the following series of letters?

    (A) verti   (B) encon   (C) verta   (D) trovr

20. The word you have just spelled contains which of the following series of letters?

    (A) olgus   (B) annallo   (C) ogous   (D) nalg

21. The word you have just spelled contains which of the following series of letters?
    (A) irras   (B) irasc   (C) sible   (D) sable

22. The word you have just spelled contains which of the following series of letters?
    (A) ellim   (B) illum   (C) illim   (D) ellum

23. The word you have just spelled contains which of the following series of letters?
    (A) ensi   (B) inci   (C) enci   (D) insi

24. The word you have just spelled contains which of the following series of letters?
    (A) tind   (B) prit   (C) tand   (D) tend

25. The word you have just spelled contains which of the following series of letters?
    (A) melli   (B) melef   (C) flus   (D) eflo

26. The word you have just spelled contains which of the following series of letters?
    (A) dible   (B) deble   (C) dable   (D) duble

27. The word you have just spelled contains which of the following series of letters?
    (A) ieva   (B) eiva   (C) ieve   (D) eive

28. The word you have just spelled contains which of the following series of letters?
    (A) awsp   (B) aucp   (C) awcp   (D) ausp

29. The word you have just spelled contains which of the following series of letters?
    (A) incon   (B) encon   (C) spick   (D) icous

30. The word you have just spelled contains which of the following series of letters?
    (A) tenate   (B) stin   (C) porcr   (D) estin

STOP   End of Test

For the Test Assistant

Oral Instructions for Following Directions Test

Directions: Wait 30 seconds after the test begins then read each question at one minute intervals. Do not repeat any questions. Stop the test at 10 minutes.

1. If you marked A for question 1, change it to B.

2. Change Row 2 to Row 3 in question 2 and change your answer if necessary.

3. Count the letters in Column 1 and 3 and select the answer in question 9, changing your original answer if necessary.

4. Reverse Column 4 and answer question 2, changing if necessary.

5. If you changed your answer to B in question 1 change it now to C.

6. If you changed your answer to question 9, change it now to reflect your original choice.

7. If you marked A in question 10 change it to C.

8. Count the number of Es in the table and answer question 10. Change your answer if necessary.

9. If you changed your answer in question 10 change it back so that it answers the original question asked.

10. Add the number of As in Column 1. From this number subtract the number of Cs in Row 5. Select your answer from the choices in question 9 and change your original answer if necessary.

Spelling Words and Sentences

Directions: Read each word and the sentence using that word. Pause 17 seconds before reading the next word to allow the test taker to answer the question. Do not repeat any word or sentence.

1. *lauded* -- Alexander Graham Bell was lauded for inventing the telephone.
2. *assimilate* -- Immigrants assimilate into the culture of their adopted country.
3. *titillation* -- Suggestive previews of movies are shown to cause titillation of the audience.
4. *reconcilable* -- Fortunately, their differences were reconcilable.
5. *assuage* -- Kind words will assuage his guilt.
6. *conspicuous* -- The Big Chicken is a conspicuous landmark.
7. *inauspicious* -- The lover returned at an inauspicious moment.
8. *virtually* -- Our team is virtually unbeatable.
9. *askew* -- Her hat sat askew upon her head.

10. *fortuitous* -- A fortuitous encounter brought them together.

11. *protuberance* -- The doctors removed the protuberance from his back.

12. *interrogate* -- The police officer will interrogate the witness.

13. *pretentious* -- His pretentious claim of noble birth was not believed.

14. *transcend* -- The feeling of love can transcend all others.

15. *incriminating* -- She did not testify for fear of incriminating herself.

16. *mystifying* -- The computer workings were mystifying to them.

17. *exemplary* -- They studied the exemplary lives of saints.

18. *immiscible* -- Oil and water are immiscible.

19. *incontrovertible* -- The evidence of his innocence was incontrovertible.

20. *analogous* -- Lungs in mammals are analogous to gills in fish.

21. *irascible* -- They were so irascible that no one wanted to work with them.

22. *illuminate* -- Search lights illuminate the building.

23. *insipid* -- The insipid conversation made her fall asleep.

24. *pretended* -- He pretended to be asleep when the salesman came to pay a visit.

25. *mellifluous* -- The chorus was noted for its mellifluous sound.

26. *laudable* -- Her goals were laudable, but her methods were not.

27. *unbelievable* -- Most reports of flying saucer encounters are unbelievable.

28. *auspicious* -- Scoring six runs in the first inning is an auspicious beginning to a baseball game.

29. *inconspicuous* -- Because of her flaming, long red hair, she was never inconspicuous.

30. *procrastinate* -- Many parents believe that teenagers are machines designed to procrastinate.

ANSWERS AND EXPLANATIONS
FOR MODEL TEST ONE

Computational Facility

1. **(A)**

$$\begin{array}{r} 2.217 \\ + .759 \\ \hline \mathbf{2.976} \end{array}$$

2. **(C)** $4,231 - 589 = \mathbf{3,642}$

3. **(D)** $\dfrac{12}{5} \div \dfrac{25}{3} = \dfrac{12}{5} \times \dfrac{3}{25} = \dfrac{\mathbf{36}}{\mathbf{125}}$

4. **(A)** $10\dfrac{3}{3} - 1\dfrac{2}{3} = \mathbf{9}\dfrac{\mathbf{1}}{\mathbf{3}}$

5. **(B)**

$$\begin{array}{r} \mathbf{259} \\ 36\overline{)\,9324} \\ \underline{72} \\ 212 \\ \underline{180} \\ 324 \\ \underline{324} \end{array}$$

6. **(C)**

54.9	45
OF	100

$54.9 \times 100 = 5490$

$5490 \div 45 = \mathbf{122}$

7. **(A)**

116.8	%
365	100

$116.8 \times 100 = 11680$

$11680 \div 365 = \mathbf{32}$

8. **(A)**   (**401.258**) Look for the answer with 3 decimal places and a last digit of 8.

9. **(D)** $\dfrac{72}{5} \times \dfrac{25}{3} = \dfrac{120}{1} = \mathbf{120}$

10. **(B)** $13\dfrac{4}{6} + 21\dfrac{1}{6} = \mathbf{34}\dfrac{\mathbf{5}}{\mathbf{6}}$

11. **(D)**

$$\begin{array}{r} 146.27 \\ - 85.88 \\ \hline \mathbf{60.39} \end{array}$$

12. **(D)**   212,769 + 14,580 = **227,349**

13. **(B)**

IS	60
84	100

84 × 60 = 5,040

5,040 ÷ 100 = **50.4**

14. **(C)** $\frac{14}{48} - \frac{9}{48} = \frac{5}{48}$

15. **(D)**

```
     .096
16)1.536
    144
     96
     96
```

16. **(C)** $\frac{9}{8} \times \frac{16}{27} = \frac{2}{3}$

17. **(A)**   93 + 25 + 24 + 16 + 45 = **203**

18. **(A)**

IS	.4
125	100

125 × .4 = 50

50 ÷ 100 = **0.5**

19. **(C)**

```
  245.600
   87.344
+  13.000
  345.944
```

20. **(D)**

```
   8392
  x  61
   8392
  50352
 511,912
```

Following Directions

1. (C)	6. (A)	11. (B)
2. (C)	7. (D)	12. (C)
3. (A)	8. (D)	13. (D)
4. (D)	9. (B)	14. (C)
5. (A)	10. (A)	15. (A)

Number Groups

1. **(A)** The third number is 2 more than the repeating number. 6646 is different because the third number is 2 less than the repeat.

2. **(C)** All the numbers are odd. 1172 is the only even number.

3. **(D)** The first pair of numbers is 10 less than the second pair. 3050 has a difference of 20.

4. **(D)** The sum of the first pair of numbers is equal to the last pair of numbers. 141448 is different because 14 plus 14 does not equal 48.

5. **(A)** There is a difference of 3 in the first and second number. There is a difference of 2 in the second and third number. 477 is different because the second number plus 2 does not equal the third number.

6. **(C)** The first three numbers in each selection are consecutive. The number 3460 is not consecutive.

7. **(C)** Each number is a combination of the numbers 2, 4, 6, 8. 5214 does not have a 6 or 8.

8. **(B)** Each number is 2 more than the previous number. 195 does not follow this pattern.

9. **(A)** The first number is 2 times the middle number. The last number is three greater than the middle number. In 634, the last number is only 1 greater.

10. **(B)** All numbers are consecutive ascending. 7654 is consecutive descending.

11. **(C)** In 6325 the last number is odd. All others are even.

12. **(B)** The three similar numbers are different combinations of 1, 7, 3. 461 does not have 7 or 3.

13. **(C)** All the numbers are consecutive ascending except 223.

14. **(D)**   Add five to the first number to find the middle number. Subtract two from the middle digit for the last number. Neither of these rules apply to 259.

15. **(A)**   All of these number series are odd. 284 is even.

16. **(B)**   The first and last numbers should be alike. The middle number has no specific pattern.

17. **(C)**   The first pair is consecutive ascending and the last numbers repeat. 4388 has a descending first pair.

18. **(A)**   All numbers begin with 920 except 9402.

19. **(D)**   The first pair is ten more than the second pair. In 4555, the first pair is ten less than the second pair.

20. **(C)**   The outside repeating numbers are two more than the inside number. In 545 the repeating numbers are one more than the inside number.

Spelling

See spelling list and sentences for correct spelling of each word.

1. (C)	11. (B)	21. (B)
2. (A)	12. (A)	22. (B)
3. (D)	13. (D)	23. (D)
4. (B)	14. (A)	24. (D)
5. (A)	15. (C)	25. (A)
6. (C)	16. (C)	26. (C)
7. (C)	17. (D)	27. (A)
8. (B)	18. (B)	28. (D)
9. (B)	19. (A)	29. (A)
10. (D)	20. (C)	30. (B)

MODEL TEST TWO ANSWER SHEET

COMPUTATIONAL FACILITY

1 Ⓐ Ⓑ Ⓒ Ⓓ	5 Ⓐ Ⓑ Ⓒ Ⓓ	9 Ⓐ Ⓑ Ⓒ Ⓓ	13 Ⓐ Ⓑ Ⓒ Ⓓ	17 Ⓐ Ⓑ Ⓒ Ⓓ
2 Ⓐ Ⓑ Ⓒ Ⓓ	6 Ⓐ Ⓑ Ⓒ Ⓓ	10 Ⓐ Ⓑ Ⓒ Ⓓ	14 Ⓐ Ⓑ Ⓒ Ⓓ	18 Ⓐ Ⓑ Ⓒ Ⓓ
3 Ⓐ Ⓑ Ⓒ Ⓓ	7 Ⓐ Ⓑ Ⓒ Ⓓ	11 Ⓐ Ⓑ Ⓒ Ⓓ	15 Ⓐ Ⓑ Ⓒ Ⓓ	19 Ⓐ Ⓑ Ⓒ Ⓓ
4 Ⓐ Ⓑ Ⓒ Ⓓ	8 Ⓐ Ⓑ Ⓒ Ⓓ	12 Ⓐ Ⓑ Ⓒ Ⓓ	16 Ⓐ Ⓑ Ⓒ Ⓓ	20 Ⓐ Ⓑ Ⓒ Ⓓ

FOLLOWING DIRECTIONS

1 Ⓐ Ⓑ Ⓒ Ⓓ	6 Ⓐ Ⓑ Ⓒ Ⓓ	11 Ⓐ Ⓑ Ⓒ Ⓓ
2 Ⓐ Ⓑ Ⓒ Ⓓ	7 Ⓐ Ⓑ Ⓒ Ⓓ	12 Ⓐ Ⓑ Ⓒ Ⓓ
3 Ⓐ Ⓑ Ⓒ Ⓓ	8 Ⓐ Ⓑ Ⓒ Ⓓ	13 Ⓐ Ⓑ Ⓒ Ⓓ
4 Ⓐ Ⓑ Ⓒ Ⓓ	9 Ⓐ Ⓑ Ⓒ Ⓓ	14 Ⓐ Ⓑ Ⓒ Ⓓ
5 Ⓐ Ⓑ Ⓒ Ⓓ	10 Ⓐ Ⓑ Ⓒ Ⓓ	15 Ⓐ Ⓑ Ⓒ Ⓓ

NUMBER GROUPS

1 Ⓐ Ⓑ Ⓒ Ⓓ	5 Ⓐ Ⓑ Ⓒ Ⓓ	9 Ⓐ Ⓑ Ⓒ Ⓓ	13 Ⓐ Ⓑ Ⓒ Ⓓ	17 Ⓐ Ⓑ Ⓒ Ⓓ
2 Ⓐ Ⓑ Ⓒ Ⓓ	6 Ⓐ Ⓑ Ⓒ Ⓓ	10 Ⓐ Ⓑ Ⓒ Ⓓ	14 Ⓐ Ⓑ Ⓒ Ⓓ	18 Ⓐ Ⓑ Ⓒ Ⓓ
3 Ⓐ Ⓑ Ⓒ Ⓓ	7 Ⓐ Ⓑ Ⓒ Ⓓ	11 Ⓐ Ⓑ Ⓒ Ⓓ	15 Ⓐ Ⓑ Ⓒ Ⓓ	19 Ⓐ Ⓑ Ⓒ Ⓓ
4 Ⓐ Ⓑ Ⓒ Ⓓ	8 Ⓐ Ⓑ Ⓒ Ⓓ	12 Ⓐ Ⓑ Ⓒ Ⓓ	16 Ⓐ Ⓑ Ⓒ Ⓓ	20 Ⓐ Ⓑ Ⓒ Ⓓ

SPELLING

1 Ⓐ Ⓑ Ⓒ Ⓓ	7 Ⓐ Ⓑ Ⓒ Ⓓ	13 Ⓐ Ⓑ Ⓒ Ⓓ	19 Ⓐ Ⓑ Ⓒ Ⓓ	25 Ⓐ Ⓑ Ⓒ Ⓓ
2 Ⓐ Ⓑ Ⓒ Ⓓ	8 Ⓐ Ⓑ Ⓒ Ⓓ	14 Ⓐ Ⓑ Ⓒ Ⓓ	20 Ⓐ Ⓑ Ⓒ Ⓓ	26 Ⓐ Ⓑ Ⓒ Ⓓ
3 Ⓐ Ⓑ Ⓒ Ⓓ	9 Ⓐ Ⓑ Ⓒ Ⓓ	15 Ⓐ Ⓑ Ⓒ Ⓓ	21 Ⓐ Ⓑ Ⓒ Ⓓ	27 Ⓐ Ⓑ Ⓒ Ⓓ
4 Ⓐ Ⓑ Ⓒ Ⓓ	10 Ⓐ Ⓑ Ⓒ Ⓓ	16 Ⓐ Ⓑ Ⓒ Ⓓ	22 Ⓐ Ⓑ Ⓒ Ⓓ	28 Ⓐ Ⓑ Ⓒ Ⓓ
5 Ⓐ Ⓑ Ⓒ Ⓓ	11 Ⓐ Ⓑ Ⓒ Ⓓ	17 Ⓐ Ⓑ Ⓒ Ⓓ	23 Ⓐ Ⓑ Ⓒ Ⓓ	29 Ⓐ Ⓑ Ⓒ Ⓓ
6 Ⓐ Ⓑ Ⓒ Ⓓ	12 Ⓐ Ⓑ Ⓒ Ⓓ	18 Ⓐ Ⓑ Ⓒ Ⓓ	24 Ⓐ Ⓑ Ⓒ Ⓓ	30 Ⓐ Ⓑ Ⓒ Ⓓ

Model Test Two

COMPUTATIONAL FACILITY

Time: 9 Minutes. 20 Questions.

This test measures the ability to do arithmetic problems accurately.

Directions: Solve each of the following mathematical operations. Mark your answers on the sample answer sheet.

1. 1,156 + 2,045 + 8,456

   (A) 11,657
   (B) 11,647
   (C) 11,557
   (D) None of the Above

2. What percent of 10 is 25?

   (A) 4 %
   (B) 40 %
   (C) 250%
   (D) None of the Above

3. 3.69×30.5

   (A) 112.545
   (B) 1125.45
   (C) 1125.45
   (D) None of the Above

4. $320\frac{1}{2} + 32\frac{1}{2}$

   (A) 353
   (B) 3530
   (C) 352 1/4
   (D) None of the Above

5. $480 \div 14$
(to the nearest tenth)

   (A) 35.0
   (B) 40.0
   (C) 34.3
   (D) None of the Above

6. 3 is what percent of 24?

   (A) 80
   (B) 8
   (C) 1.25
   (D) None of the Above

7. 15% of what is 75?

(A) 200

(B) 500

(C) 5

(D) None of the Above

8. 97.24×3.001

(A) 291.09724

(B) 291817.24

(C) 291.81724

(D) None of the Above

9. $8\frac{1}{2} \div 2\frac{5}{6}$

(A) 3

(B) 2 14/17

(C) 4

(D) None of the Above

10. 201.8 - 30.217

(A) 231.617

(B) 171.617

(C) 171.583

(D) None of the Above

11. 1001 - 208

(A) 803

(B) 793

(C) 703

(D) None of the Above

12. $99 - 10\frac{2}{5}$

(A) 89 3/5

(B) 89 2/5

(C) 88 2/5

(D) None of the Above

13. What is 80% of 64?

(A) 512

(B) 5.12

(C) 5120

(D) None of the Above

14. $17\frac{5}{7}+8\frac{3}{14}$

(A) 25 8/14
(B) 25 13/14
(C) 26 1/7
(D) None of the Above

15. $87,906 \div 897$

(A) 103
(B) 97
(C) 98
(D) None of the Above

16. $2\frac{2}{7}\times 3\frac{1}{2}$

(A) 6 1/7
(B) 8
(C) 6 2/14
(D) None of the Above

17. $103 + 25 + 34 + 27 + 65$

(A) 244
(B) 254
(C) 264
(D) None of the Above

18. What is 14% of 100?

(A) 140
(B) 14
(C) 1.4
(D) None of the Above

19. $345.3 + 42.304 + 3$

(A) 387.904
(B) 387.604
(C) 390.604
(D) None of the Above

20. 164×37

(A) 6068
(B) 6086
(C) 5048
(D) None of the Above

FOLLOWING DIRECTIONS

Time: 10 Minutes. 15 Questions.

This test measures your ability to follow both written and oral instructions.

Directions: Use the table below to follow the written and oral directions. Mark your answers on the sample answer sheet.

To the Test Assistant: Turn to page 143 for the oral instructions. If you do not have someone to read the oral directions for you, record them yourself and play them back when you begin the exam.

	Column				
	1	2	3	4	5
Row 1	B	D	E	B	A
Row 2	E	D	A	B	E
Row 3	A	B	C	D	E
Row 4	C	B	D	B	C
Row 5	A	C	E	B	E

1. Find the letter in Row 2 Column 4.

　(A) A　　(B) B　　(C) D　　(D) E

2. Which letter does not appear in the chart?

　(A) B　　(B) D　　(C) F　　(D) E

3. Which letter is in the middle of the chart?

　(A) A　　(B) C　　(C) D　　(D) E

4. What is the total number of letters in Column 4 and Row 5?

　(A) 9　　(B) 10　　(C) 15　　(D) 25

5. Which letter is most frequently just below A?

　(A) B　　(B) C　　(C) D　　(D) E

6. Which letter is first in more than one row?

    (A) A   (B) B   (C) C   (D) D

7. Which column contains only two different letters?

    (A) 1   (B) 2   (C) 3   (D) 4

8. Which letter appears twice in Column 3?

    (A) E   (B) D   (C) C   (D) A

9. Which letter appears in Column 5 Row 4?

    (A) A   (B) B   (C) C   (D) D

10. Which row contains five different letters?

    (A) 1   (B) 3   (C) 5   (D) 2

11. If Row 1 was reversed, what letter would be just below the letter just below the letter to the left of the letter B in Column 5?

    (A) A   (B) B   (C) C   (D) D

12. How many times does the letter B appear in the table?

    (A) 4   (B) 5   (C) 6   (D) 7

13. What letter is two spaces to the right of the letter that is just above the letter that is to the left of the next to the last letter in Row 2?

    (A) A   (B) C   (C) D   (D) E

14. If Row 2 was reversed, and Row 4 was reversed, which Column would contain the most Ds?

    (A) 1   (B) 2   (C) 3   (D) 4

15. If Columns 1 and 5 were reversed, what letter would be just above the letter just to the right of the letter just above the letter just to the left of the letter in Row 3, Column 5?

    (A) A   (B) C   (C) D   (D) E

NUMBER GROUPS

Time: 7 Minutes. 20 Questions.

This is a test of your ability to see how groups of numbers are alike or different.

Directions: _Each problem has four groups of numbers; three of the number groups have something in common. Darken the choice on your sample answer sheet that corresponds to the one group that is different from the other three._

1.	(A) 234	(B) 426	(C) 336	(D) 538
2.	(A) 322	(B) 954	(C) 514	(D) 734
3.	(A) 1805	(B) 1905	(C) 1305	(D) 1955
4.	(A) 282	(B) 121	(C) 242	(D) 363
5.	(A) 8338	(B) 5225	(C) 6116	(D) 7227
6.	(A) 1155	(B) 2266	(C) 3377	(D) 6688
7.	(A) 2222	(B) 7777	(C) 6666	(D) 4444
8.	(A) 802	(B) 374	(C) 897	(D) 106
9.	(A) 603	(B) 522	(C) 342	(D) 453
10.	(A) 404	(B) 303	(C) 505	(D) 212
11.	(A) 3851	(B) 4583	(C) 8513	(D) 1385
12.	(A) 4321	(B) 6543	(C) 5678	(D) 9876
13.	(A) 6422	(B) 7522	(C) 9622	(D) 5322
14.	(A) 9918	(B) 8816	(C) 5510	(D) 6614
15.	(A) 1325	(B) 3258	(C) 8325	(D) 3852
16.	(A) 6012	(B) 7021	(C) 8024	(D) 5015
17.	(A) 8602	(B) 8603	(C) 8608	(D) 8604
18.	(A) 4015	(B) 3510	(C) 5025	(D) 6030
19.	(A) 4554	(B) 3223	(C) 7887	(D) 8998
20.	(A) 7580	(B) 5055	(C) 4035	(D) 2530

SPELLING

Time: 12 Minutes. 30 Questions.

This test measures your ability to spell words correctly.

Directions: For each question a test assistant will pronounce a word to be spelled and then use it in a sentence. On your answer sheet, mark the letter series from the answer choices that is contained in the correct spelling of the word. If you do not have someone to read the words, record them yourself and play them back when you begin the test.

To the Test Assistant: Turn to pages 143-144 for the spelling list and corresponding sentences.

1. The word you have just spelled contains which of the following series of letters?

    (A) rrough   (B) rought   (C) rawt   (D) raught

2. The word you have just spelled contains which of the following series of letters?

    (A) stir   (B) boys   (C) bois   (D) trous

3. The word you have just spelled contains which of the following series of letters?

    (A) pore   (B) rapp   (C) pour   (D) rapo

4. The word you have just spelled contains which of the following series of letters?

    (A) essti   (B) oses   (C) osses   (D) sesi

5. The word you have just spelled contains which of the following series of letters?

    (A) ieter   (B) eitor   (C) ryet   (D) ietor

6. The word you have just spelled contains which of the following series of letters?

    (A) spik   (B) spico   (C) cuous   (D) cous

7. The word you have just spelled contains which of the following series of letters?

    (A) nsend   (B) scend   (C) dant   (D) senda

8. The word you have just spelled contains which of the following series of letters?

    (A) mita   (B) mett   (C) tten   (D) mitt

9. The word you have just spelled contains which of the following series of letters?

(A) billi   (B) sept   (C) scept   (D) tabi

10. The word you have just spelled contains which of the following series of letters?

(A) trou   (B) trau   (C) traw   (D) trow

11. The word you have just spelled contains which of the following series of letters?

(A) rett   (B) retis   (C) sens   (D) cenc

12. The word you have just spelled contains which of the following series of letters?

(A) fali   (B) fall   (C) able   (D) libe

13. The word you have just spelled contains which of the following series of letters?

(A) etion   (B) ashun   (C) ation   (D) aton

14. The word you have just spelled contains which of the following series of letters?

(A) isea   (B) cear   (C) ciar   (D) ishi

15. The word you have just spelled contains which of the following series of letters?

(A) llema   (B) dell   (C) emma   (D) dill

16. The word you have just spelled contains which of the following series of letters?

(A) rech   (B) wret   (C) retc   (D) ache

17. The word you have just spelled contains which of the following series of letters?

(A) dicr   (B) dikr   (C) dekr   (D) decr

18. The word you have just spelled contains which of the following series of letters?

(A) lemi   (B) limi   (C) lema   (D) lima

19. The word you have just spelled contains which of the following series of letters?

(A) artica   (B) artick   (C) artik   (D) articu

20. The word you have just spelled contains which of the following series of letters?

(A) tina   (B) tena   (C) tious   (D) sious

21. The word you have just spelled contains which of the following series of letters?

(A) magez   (B) mages   (C) magaz   (D) magas

22. The word you have just spelled contains which of the following series of letters?

(A) inaw   (B) awga   (C) aurg   (D) augu

23. The word you have just spelled contains which of the following series of letters?

(A) kwis   (B) lenq   (C) qish   (D) nqui

24. The word you have just spelled contains which of the following series of letters?

(A) exxo   (B) exon   (C) nare   (D) reted

25. The word you have just spelled contains which of the following series of letters?

(A) krep   (B) penc   (C) desc   (D) panc

26. The word you have just spelled contains which of the following series of letters?

(A) tance   (B) tence   (C) purs   (D) tanse

27. The word you have just spelled contains which of the following series of letters?

(A) rise   (B) aver   (C) avar   (D) riss

28. The word you have just spelled contains which of the following series of letters?

(A) fict   (B) fick   (C) tish   (D) shous

29. The word you have just spelled contains which of the following series of letters?

(A) cama   (B) flaw   (C) camou   (D) flah

30. The word you have just spelled contains which of the following series of letters?

(A) sory   (B) compel   (C) cumpu   (D) sery

STOP | End of Test

For the Test Assistant

Oral Instructions

Directions: Wait 30 seconds after the test begins then read each question at one minute intervals. Do not repeat any questions. Stop the test at 10 minutes.

1. If you marked answer C for question 1, change your answer to A.

2. If you marked D for question 2, change your answer to C.

3. Reverse Row 3 and then go back and answer question 3. Change your answer if necessary.

4. Change number 2 to number 3 in question 1, change your answer if necessary.

5. Reverse Column 3 for question 9, change your answer if necessary.

6. If you marked C for question 7 change it to B.

7. If you changed your answer in question 1, change it now to D.

8. If you changed your answer in question 9, change it back so that it answers the original question.

9. Change Column 3 to Row 5 in number 8. Change your answer if necessary.

10. If you marked C in question 13, change it to A.

Spelling Words and Sentences

Directions: Read each word and the sentence using that word. Pause 17 seconds before reading the next word to allow the test taker to answer the question. Do not repeat any word or sentence.

1. *overwrought* -- She was overwrought with grief from the loss of her husband.

2. *boisterous* -- The boisterous diners annoyed the woman at the next table.

3. *rapport* -- The teacher had good rapport with her students.

4. *possession* -- He was in possession of several valuable paintings.

5. *proprietor* -- The overweight bakery proprietor looks like he eats more pastry than he sells.

6. *conspicuous* -- The red dress made her conspicuous in the crowd.

7. *transcendent* -- Many religious beliefs are said to be transcendent because they exist above and independent of the material universe.

8. *remittance* -- Please forward a remittance for the expense of the delivery.

9. *susceptibility* -- The unvaccinated child had a susceptibility to measles.

10. *traumatic* -- Taking a test is a traumatic experience for most people.

11. *reticence* -- She overcame her reticence and spoke out in the meeting.

12. *infallible* -- The Jeopardy contestant answered every question correctly. He seemed infallible.

13. *deviation* -- The ship's deviation from its course was so slight that none of the passengers noticed.

14. *beneficiary* -- The beneficiary of his estate will receive a small fortune.

15. *dilemma* -- Whether or not to finish school is a dilemma many students find hard to resolve.

16. *treacherous* -- The slippery rocks made the trail treacherous.

17. *decrepit* -- The decrepit old man stood on the corner begging for change.

18. *limitation* -- There is no limitation to what a determined person can achieve.

19. *articulate* -- Newscasters articulate their words very clearly.

20. *tenacious* -- They were tenacious in their pursuit of freedom.

21. *magazine* -- The magazine subscription expires this month.

22. *inauguration* -- The presidential inauguration occurs every four years.

23. *relinquish* -- The loser was reluctant to relinquish the title.

24. *exonerated* -- After a lengthy trial, the accused was exonerated from all charges.

25. *discrepancy* -- There was no discrepancy in the grading procedures for the test.

26. *persistence* -- Her persistence was rewarded with financial gain.

27. *avarice* -- Avarice is another word for greed.

28. *fictitious* -- All the characters in the movie were fictitious.

29. *camouflage* -- Natural camouflage protects many insects from being eaten by predators.

30. *compulsory* -- Sometimes it seems that everything is either forbidden or compulsory.

ANSWERS AND EXPLANATIONS
FOR MODEL TEST TWO

Computational Facility

1. **(A)**
$$\begin{array}{r} 1156 \\ 2045 \\ + 8456 \\ \hline \mathbf{11{,}657} \end{array}$$

2. **(C)**

25	%
10	100

$100 \times 25 = 2{,}500$

$2500 \div 10 = \mathbf{250}$

3. **(A)**
$$\begin{array}{r} 3.69 \\ \times\ 30.5 \\ \hline 1845 \\ 000 \\ 1107 \\ \hline \mathbf{112.545} \end{array}$$

4. **(A)**
$$320\frac{1}{2} + 32\frac{1}{2} = 352\frac{2}{2} = 352 + 1 = \mathbf{353}$$

5. **(C)**
$$\begin{array}{r} 34.28 \\ 14{\overline{)480.00}} \\ \underline{42} \\ 60 \\ \underline{56} \\ 4\ 0 \\ \underline{2\ 8} \\ 1\ 20 \\ \underline{1\ 12} \end{array}$$
Rounded to the nearest tenth yields an answer of **34.3**

6. **(D)**

3	%
24	100

$100 \times 3 = 300$

$300 \div 24 = \mathbf{12.5}$

7. **(B)**

75	15
OF	100

$100 \times 75 = 7{,}500$

$7500 \div 15 = \mathbf{500}$

8. (C)
$$
\begin{array}{r}
97.24 \\
\times\ 3.001 \\
\hline
9724 \\
0000 \\
0000 \\
29172 \\
\hline
291.81724
\end{array}
$$

9. (A)
$$\frac{17}{2} \div \frac{17}{6} = \frac{17}{2} \times \frac{6}{17} = \frac{3}{1} = 3$$

10. (C)
$$
\begin{array}{r}
201.800 \\
-\ 30.217 \\
\hline
171.583
\end{array}
$$

11. (B)
$$
\begin{array}{r}
1001 \\
-\ 208 \\
\hline
793
\end{array}
$$

12. (D)
$$99 - 10\frac{2}{5} = 98\frac{5}{5} - 10\frac{2}{5} = 88\frac{3}{5}$$

13. (D)

IS	80
64	100

$80 \times 64 = 5,120$

$5,120 \div 100 = 51.2$

14. (B)
$$17\frac{5}{7} + 8\frac{3}{14} = 17\frac{10}{14} + 8\frac{3}{14} = 25\frac{13}{14}$$

15. (C)
$$
\begin{array}{r}
98 \\
897\,\overline{)\,87906} \\
8073 \\
\hline
7176 \\
7176 \\
\hline
\end{array}
$$

16. (B)
$$\frac{16}{7} \times \frac{7}{2} = \frac{8}{1} = 8$$

17. (B)
$$
\begin{array}{r}
103 \\
25 \\
34 \\
27 \\
+\ 65 \\
\hline
254
\end{array}
$$

18. **(B)**

IS	14
100	100

$14 \times 100 = 1,400$

$1400 \div 100 = \mathbf{14}$

19. **(C)**
```
  345.300
   42.304
+   3.000
  390.604
```

20. **(A)**
```
   164
 x  37
  1148
  492
  6068
```

Following Directions

1. **(D)**
2. **(C)**
3. **(B)**
4. **(A)**
5. **(B)**
6. **(A)**
7. **(D)**
8. **(A)**
9. **(C)**
10. **(B)**
11. **(D)**
12. **(D)**
13. **(A)**
14. **(D)**
15. **(D)**

Number Groups

1. **(A)** The sum of the first and second number is equal to the 3rd number. 234 is different because 2 + 3 does not equal 4.

2. **(A)** The sum of the second and last number is equal to the first number. 322 is different because 2 + 2 does not equal 3.

3. **(D)** The last numbers are 05. 1955 is different because the last two numbers are 55 instead of 05.

4. **(A)** The sum of the outside numbers equals the inside number. 2 + 2 does not equal 8.

5. **(B)** The difference between the first and second number is 5. 8 - 3 = 5 in 8338. 5 - 2 does not equal 5 in 5225.

6. **(D)** The first repeat is 4 less than the last repeat. 6688 is two less than its last repeat.

7. **(B)** 7777 is different because it is an odd numbered repeat.

8. **(C)**   897 is odd.

9. **(D)**   All the digits of each number add up to 9. 6 + 3 = 9,
5 + 2 + 2 = 9 but 4 + 5 + 3 = 12 not 9.

10. **(D)**   The middle number is zero. 212 is different because the middle number is 1 not zero.

11. **(B)**   Each number is a different arrangement of the numbers 1, 3, 5, and 8. 4583 does not have a 1.

12. **(C)**   The numbers are consecutive descending. 5678 is a consecutive ascending number.

13. **(C)**   The first number minus the second number equals 2. 9 - 6 = 3 not 2, so 9622 is different.

14. **(D)**   The first number plus the second number equals the last 2 numbers. 6614 is different because 6 + 6 = 12 not 14.

15. **(A)**   Each number is a different arrangement of the numbers 2, 3, 5, 8. 1325 does not have an 8.

16. **(A)**   The first number multiplied by 3 is equal to the last pair of numbers. 6012 is different because 6 x 3 = 18 not 12.

17. **(B)**   The number 8603 is odd while the other three are even.

18. **(D)**   The first pair of numbers minus 25 is equal to the last pair of numbers. 6030 is different because 60 - 25 equals 35 not 30.

19. **(B)**   The inside repeating number is one more than the outside repeating number. 3223 is different because the inside is one less than the outside number.

20. **(C)**   The first pair of numbers plus five equals the last pair. 4035 is different because 40 plus 5 is 45, not 35.

Spelling

1. (B)	6. (C)	11. (D)	16. (D)	21. (C)	26. (B)
2. (C)	7. (B)	12. (B)	17. (D)	22. (D)	27. (C)
3. (B)	8. (D)	13. (C)	18. (B)	23. (D)	28. (A)
4. (C)	9. (C)	14. (C)	19. (D)	24. (B)	29. (C)
5. (D)	10. (B)	15. (C)	20. (B)	25. (D)	30. (A)

MODEL TEST THREE ANSWER SHEET

COMPUTATIONAL FACILITY

1 Ⓐ Ⓑ Ⓒ Ⓓ	5 Ⓐ Ⓑ Ⓒ Ⓓ	9 Ⓐ Ⓑ Ⓒ Ⓓ	13 Ⓐ Ⓑ Ⓒ Ⓓ	17 Ⓐ Ⓑ Ⓒ Ⓓ
2 Ⓐ Ⓑ Ⓒ Ⓓ	6 Ⓐ Ⓑ Ⓒ Ⓓ	10 Ⓐ Ⓑ Ⓒ Ⓓ	14 Ⓐ Ⓑ Ⓒ Ⓓ	18 Ⓐ Ⓑ Ⓒ Ⓓ
3 Ⓐ Ⓑ Ⓒ Ⓓ	7 Ⓐ Ⓑ Ⓒ Ⓓ	11 Ⓐ Ⓑ Ⓒ Ⓓ	15 Ⓐ Ⓑ Ⓒ Ⓓ	19 Ⓐ Ⓑ Ⓒ Ⓓ
4 Ⓐ Ⓑ Ⓒ Ⓓ	8 Ⓐ Ⓑ Ⓒ Ⓓ	12 Ⓐ Ⓑ Ⓒ Ⓓ	16 Ⓐ Ⓑ Ⓒ Ⓓ	20 Ⓐ Ⓑ Ⓒ Ⓓ

FOLLOWING DIRECTIONS

1 Ⓐ Ⓑ Ⓒ Ⓓ	6 Ⓐ Ⓑ Ⓒ Ⓓ	11 Ⓐ Ⓑ Ⓒ Ⓓ
2 Ⓐ Ⓑ Ⓒ Ⓓ	7 Ⓐ Ⓑ Ⓒ Ⓓ	12 Ⓐ Ⓑ Ⓒ Ⓓ
3 Ⓐ Ⓑ Ⓒ Ⓓ	8 Ⓐ Ⓑ Ⓒ Ⓓ	13 Ⓐ Ⓑ Ⓒ Ⓓ
4 Ⓐ Ⓑ Ⓒ Ⓓ	9 Ⓐ Ⓑ Ⓒ Ⓓ	14 Ⓐ Ⓑ Ⓒ Ⓓ
5 Ⓐ Ⓑ Ⓒ Ⓓ	10 Ⓐ Ⓑ Ⓒ Ⓓ	15 Ⓐ Ⓑ Ⓒ Ⓓ

NUMBER GROUPS

1 Ⓐ Ⓑ Ⓒ Ⓓ	5 Ⓐ Ⓑ Ⓒ Ⓓ	9 Ⓐ Ⓑ Ⓒ Ⓓ	13 Ⓐ Ⓑ Ⓒ Ⓓ	17 Ⓐ Ⓑ Ⓒ Ⓓ
2 Ⓐ Ⓑ Ⓒ Ⓓ	6 Ⓐ Ⓑ Ⓒ Ⓓ	10 Ⓐ Ⓑ Ⓒ Ⓓ	14 Ⓐ Ⓑ Ⓒ Ⓓ	18 Ⓐ Ⓑ Ⓒ Ⓓ
3 Ⓐ Ⓑ Ⓒ Ⓓ	7 Ⓐ Ⓑ Ⓒ Ⓓ	11 Ⓐ Ⓑ Ⓒ Ⓓ	15 Ⓐ Ⓑ Ⓒ Ⓓ	19 Ⓐ Ⓑ Ⓒ Ⓓ
4 Ⓐ Ⓑ Ⓒ Ⓓ	8 Ⓐ Ⓑ Ⓒ Ⓓ	12 Ⓐ Ⓑ Ⓒ Ⓓ	16 Ⓐ Ⓑ Ⓒ Ⓓ	20 Ⓐ Ⓑ Ⓒ Ⓓ

SPELLING

1 Ⓐ Ⓑ Ⓒ Ⓓ	7 Ⓐ Ⓑ Ⓒ Ⓓ	13 Ⓐ Ⓑ Ⓒ Ⓓ	19 Ⓐ Ⓑ Ⓒ Ⓓ	25 Ⓐ Ⓑ Ⓒ Ⓓ
2 Ⓐ Ⓑ Ⓒ Ⓓ	8 Ⓐ Ⓑ Ⓒ Ⓓ	14 Ⓐ Ⓑ Ⓒ Ⓓ	20 Ⓐ Ⓑ Ⓒ Ⓓ	26 Ⓐ Ⓑ Ⓒ Ⓓ
3 Ⓐ Ⓑ Ⓒ Ⓓ	9 Ⓐ Ⓑ Ⓒ Ⓓ	15 Ⓐ Ⓑ Ⓒ Ⓓ	21 Ⓐ Ⓑ Ⓒ Ⓓ	27 Ⓐ Ⓑ Ⓒ Ⓓ
4 Ⓐ Ⓑ Ⓒ Ⓓ	10 Ⓐ Ⓑ Ⓒ Ⓓ	16 Ⓐ Ⓑ Ⓒ Ⓓ	22 Ⓐ Ⓑ Ⓒ Ⓓ	28 Ⓐ Ⓑ Ⓒ Ⓓ
5 Ⓐ Ⓑ Ⓒ Ⓓ	11 Ⓐ Ⓑ Ⓒ Ⓓ	17 Ⓐ Ⓑ Ⓒ Ⓓ	23 Ⓐ Ⓑ Ⓒ Ⓓ	29 Ⓐ Ⓑ Ⓒ Ⓓ
6 Ⓐ Ⓑ Ⓒ Ⓓ	12 Ⓐ Ⓑ Ⓒ Ⓓ	18 Ⓐ Ⓑ Ⓒ Ⓓ	24 Ⓐ Ⓑ Ⓒ Ⓓ	30 Ⓐ Ⓑ Ⓒ Ⓓ

Model Test Three

COMPUTATIONAL FACILITY

Time: 9 Minutes. 20 Questions.

This test measures the ability to do arithmetic problems accurately.

Directions: *Solve each of the following mathematical operations. Mark your answers on the sample answer sheet.*

1. 60% of what number is 120?
   (A) 50
   (B) 500
   (C) 200
   (D) None of the Above

2. 987 + 135
   (A) 1122
   (B) 1112
   (C) 1212
   (D) None of the Above

3. 3768×547
   (A) 2,061,095
   (B) 2,061,086
   (C) 2,060,986
   (D) None of the Above

4. 98,356 - 79,398
   (A) 8962
   (B) 18,958
   (C) 18,946
   (D) None of the Above

5. $5\frac{3}{4} + 7\frac{1}{3}$
   (A) 13
   (B) 13 1/12
   (C) 12 1/12
   (D) None of the Above

6. 98,354 - 97,589

- (A) 765
- (B) 775
- (C) 755
- (D) None of the Above

7. $4\frac{1}{6} \div 6\frac{4}{5}$

- (A) 28 1/3
- (B) 125/204
- (C) 24 2/15
- (D) None of the Above

8. 89,396 + 30,105

- (A) 119,491
- (B) 119,501
- (C) 119,511
- (D) None of the Above

9. What is 5.8% of 220?

- (A) 128
- (B) 37.93
- (C) 12.76
- (D) None of the Above

10. $\frac{8}{11} \times \frac{3}{4}$

- (A) 32/33
- (B) 3/11
- (C) 24/44
- (D) None of the Above

11. 5984 ÷ 17

- (A) 352
- (B) 292
- (C) 342
- (D) None of the Above

12. 5.6 + .084 + .15

- (A) 5.695
- (B) 0.5834
- (C) 20.684
- (D) None of the Above

13. 64 is what percent of 512?

- (A) 12
- (B) 12 1/2
- (C) 16
- (D) None of the Above

14. $15\frac{1}{9} - 7\frac{5}{6}$

(A) 7 5/18
(B) 8 5/18
(C) 6 5/18
(D) None of the Above

15. 87.36 ÷ 5.2

(A) 168
(B) 1.68
(C) 6.8
(D) None of the Above

16. 89.3 - 17.358

(A) 72.058
(B) 72.042
(C) 71.942
(D) None of the Above

17. 3.05 × 9.2

(A) 28.06
(B) 28.006
(C) 2.806
(D) None of the Above

18. 156 × 79

(A) 12,324
(B) 11,234
(C) 11,324
(D) None of the Above

19. 14.62 ÷ 17

(A) 1.16
(B) .86
(C) 116
(D) None of the Above

20. What is 35% of 450?

(A) 12.9
(B) 151.5
(C) 157.5
(D) None of the Above

FOLLOWING DIRECTIONS

Time: 10 Minutes. 15 Questions.

This test measures your ability to follow both written and oral instructions.

<u>Directions</u>: Use the table below to follow the written and oral directions. Mark your answers on the sample answer sheet.

<u>To the Test Assistant</u>: Turn to page 161 for the oral instructions. If you do not have someone to read the oral directions for you, record them yourself and play them back when you begin the exam.

	Column					
	M	N	O	P	Q	R
Row M	1	4	6	1	2	3
Row N	2	7	5	2	3	1
Row O	1	3	4	5	4	2
Row P	7	4	5	1	3	5
Row Q	6	7	4	2	6	7

1. What number does not appear in the table?

    (A) 2   (B) 4   (C) 6   (D) 8

2. Find the number on Row M Column Q.

    (A) 2   (B) 6   (C) 1   (D) 3

3. What number is always just above 2?

    (A) 1   (B) 3   (C) 5   (D) 7

4. How many different numbers are in the table?

    (A) 5   (B) 6   (C) 7   (D) 8

5. What is the sum of the numbers in Column P?

    (A) 20   (B) 11   (C) 10   (D) 25

6. How many columns are there?

   (A) 5   (B) 6   (C) 7   (D) 8

7. How many times does the number 7 appear in the table?

   (A) 2   (B) 3   (C) 4   (D) 5

8. Which column has only 3 different numbers?

   (A) Q   (B) R   (C) N   (D) M

9. Which number appears twice in Row Q?

   (A) 6   (B) 2   (C) 3   (D) 4

10. Find the number in Row P and Column O.

    (A) 5   (B) 4   (C) 3   (D) 2

11. If Row M was reversed, what number would be just below the number to the right of the number 6?

    (A) 1   (B) 3   (C) 5   (D) 2

12. Locate the row that does not have a number 1.

    (A) N   (B) O   (C) P   (D) Q

13. If Rows N and P were reversed, what number would be just below the number just to the left of the number just below the number just to the right of the number in Row N, Column P?

    (A) 1   (B) 3   (C) 4   (D) 5

14. If Column M was reversed and Column R was reversed, which Row would contain the least number of ones (1)?

    (A) M   (B) N   (C) O   (D) P

15. What number is 3 spaces to the left of the number that is just above the number that is to the left of the last number in Row Q?

    (A) 1   (B) 3   (C) 6   (D) 4

NUMBER GROUPS

Time: 7 Minutes. 20 Questions.

This is a test of your ability to see how groups of numbers are alike or different.

Directions: *Each problem has four groups of numbers; three of the number groups have something in common. Darken the space on your sample answer sheet that corresponds to the one group that is different from the other three.*

1.	(A) 1234	(B) 5678	(C) 3456	(D) 5432
2.	(A) 1000	(B) 0100	(C) 0001	(D) 1001
3.	(A) 1355	(B) 2876	(C) 9873	(D) 8239
4.	(A) 189	(B) 268	(C) 195	(D) 246
5.	(A) 5345	(B) 6786	(C) 9569	(D) 4874
6.	(A) 9581	(B) 7431	(C) 8351	(D) 6421
7.	(A) 818	(B) 428	(C) 520	(D) 326
8.	(A) 7007	(B) 3003	(C) 4004	(D) 9009
9.	(A) 1543	(B) 4543	(C) 9543	(D) 7543
10.	(A) 1357	(B) 3579	(C) 4682	(D) 2468
11.	(A) 1919	(B) 1818	(C) 1411	(D) 1616
12.	(A) 8765	(B) 4321	(C) 7654	(D) 6543
13.	(A) 1520	(B) 5065	(C) 4560	(D) 2035
14.	(A) 532	(B) 515	(C) 743	(D) 633
15.	(A) 8976	(B) 7869	(C) 9678	(D) 9685
16.	(A) 7134	(B) 6115	(C) 9189	(D) 6126
17.	(A) 2222	(B) 7777	(C) 4444	(D) 9666
18.	(A) 9555	(B) 6224	(C) 7333	(D) 8444
19.	(A) 2200	(B) 4400	(C) 6600	(D) 1100
20.	(A) 540	(B) 630	(C) 910	(D) 720

SPELLING

Time: 12 Minutes. 30 Questions.

This test measures your ability to spell words correctly.

<u>Directions:</u> *For each question a test assistant will pronounce a word to be spelled and then use it in a sentence. On your answer sheet, mark the letter series from the answer choices that is contained in the correct spelling of the word. If you do not have someone to read the words, record them yourself and play them back when you begin the test.*

<u>To the Test Assistant:</u> *Turn to pages 161-162 for the spelling list and corresponding sentences.*

1. The word you have just spelled contains which of the following series of letters?

    (A) ostint   (B) ostent   (C) facious   (D) tasious

2. The word you have just spelled contains which of the following series of letters?

    (A) fisie   (B) fisie   (C) fisei   (D) cienc

3. The word you have just spelled contains which of the following series of letters?

    (A) curing   (B) curring   (C) corring   (D) coring

4. The word you have just spelled contains which of the following series of letters?

    (A) traor   (B) trord   (C) treord   (D) trard

5. The word you have just spelled contains which of the following series of letters?

    (A) hipote   (B) hipoth   (C) hypot   (D) hypat

6. The word you have just spelled contains which of the following series of letters?

    (A) litha   (B) lethr   (C) letar   (D) lethar

7. The word you have just spelled contains which of the following series of letters?

    (A) dace   (B) deci   (C) dece   (D) daci

8. The word you have just spelled contains which of the following series of letters?

    (A) cour   (B) corag   (C) gous   (D) agus

9. The word you have just spelled contains which of the following series of letters?

    (A) rible   (B) sera   (C) rabel   (D) rble

10. The word you have just spelled contains which of the following series of letters?

    (A) exas   (B) ecsa   (C) exsa   (D) spar

11. The word you have just spelled contains which of the following series of letters?

    (A) ello   (B) quin   (C) quen   (D) elow

12. The word you have just spelled contains which of the following series of letters?

    (A) tible   (B) table   (C) etible   (D) etibel

13. The word you have just spelled contains which of the following series of letters?

    (A) lejer   (B) belig   (C) belli   (D) lijer

14. The word you have just spelled contains which of the following series of letters?

    (A) teckn   (B) tecni   (C) tekni   (D) techn

15. The word you have just spelled contains which of the following series of letters?

    (A) illeg   (B) illig   (C) ilege   (D) ellegi

16. The word you have just spelled contains which of the following series of letters?

    (A) series   (B) ceries   (C) caries   (D) saries

17. The word you have just spelled contains which of the following series of letters?

    (A) etius   (B) etous   (C) itious   (D) etious

18. The word you have just spelled contains which of the following series of letters?

    (A) shal   (B) chal   (C) tial   (D) ntal

19. The word you have just spelled contains which of the following series of letters?

    (A) orete   (B) orate   (C) erate   (D) arate

20. The word you have just spelled contains which of the following series of letters?

    (A) dgem   (B) dgme   (C) djme   (D) ugme

21. The word you have just spelled contains which of the following series of letters?

(A) enoc   (B) inoc   (C) inos   (D) inno

22. The word you have just spelled contains which of the following series of letters?

(A) caly   (B) cally   (C) icly   (D) cley

23. The word you have just spelled contains which of the following series of letters?

(A) fering   (B) furing   (C) ferring   (D) farring

24. The word you have just spelled contains which of the following series of letters?

(A) comme   (B) comen   (C) omenn   (D) ommenn

25. The word you have just spelled contains which of the following series of letters?

(A) vale   (B) vele   (C) vile   (D) vila

26. The word you have just spelled contains which of the following series of letters?

(A) menis   (B) mines   (C) minis   (D) stras

27. The word you have just spelled contains which of the following series of letters?

(A) cense   (B) sence   (C) cents   (D) sents

28. The word you have just spelled contains which of the following series of letters?

(A) spable   (B) sabel   (C) pensa   (D) penca

29. The word you have just spelled contains which of the following series of letters?

(A) quelo   (B) ridec   (C) ridic   (D) culus

30. The word you have just spelled contains which of the following series of letters?

(A) nshal   (B) ntle   (C) ntel   (D) ntial

STOP   End of Test

For the Test Assistant

Oral Instructions

Directions: *Wait 30 seconds after the test begins then read each question at one minute intervals. Do not repeat any questions. Stop the test at 10 minutes.*

1. If you answered D for question 1, change it to A.

2. In question 2, change Row M to Row N and change your answer if necessary.

3. If you answered C for question 1, change it to A.

4. In question 7 change 7 to 5 and answer the question accordingly.

5. If you answered B for question 9 change it to A.

6. In question 5 change the word column to row and change your answer if necessary.

7. If you changed your answer to question 1, change it back so that it answers the original question.

8. In question 12 change the word row to column and the number 1 to 4, and change your answer if necessary.

9. Answer question 11 but do not reverse Row M.

10. If your last answer to question 11 was B, change it to A.

Spelling Words and Sentences

Directions: *Read each word and the sentence using that word. Pause 17 seconds before reading the next word to allow the test taker to answer the question. Do not repeat any word or sentence.*

1. *ostentatious* -- He wears the most ostentatious jewelry.

2. *proficiency* -- You must show proficiency in the course before you can graduate.

3. *recurring* -- The recurring dream frightened the child.

4. *extraordinary* -- It requires extraordinary balance to walk a tightrope.

5. *hypothetical* -- Let me ask you a hypothetical question.

6. *lethargic* -- Illness and overwork reduced him to a lethargic state.

7. *deceitful* -- Do you suppose car salespersons are born deceitful or is it an acquired trait?

8. *courageous* -- Love made the soldiers more courageous.

9. *miserable* -- The sunburn on her back caused miserable camping.

10. *exasperated* -- The thoughtless children exasperated their mother.

11. *eloquence* -- The speaker's eloquence may mask his weak argument.

12. *perceptible* -- The tiny figure was barely perceptible 500 yards away.

13. *belligerent* -- They crossed the street to avoid the belligerent drunk.

14. *technical* -- This technical bulletin describes the operation of these machines.

15. *illegible* -- I cannot read your illegible handwriting.

16. *adversaries* -- They were friends at work but adversaries on the basketball court.

17. *facetious* -- Her facetious remarks brought smiles to the audience.

18. *confidential* -- This confidential memo must not be seen by the press.

19. *elaborate* -- That was an elaborate costume you wore to the ball.

20. *judgment* -- It is the judgment of the court that you are innocent.

21. *innocence* -- The jury was never in doubt of her innocence.

22. *practically* -- The mall is practically deserted on weekdays.

23. *transferring* -- She is transferring all her files to the new office.

24. *recommendation* -- It is my recommendation that we stop production.

25. *privilege* -- It is a privilege to have the opportunity to meet with you.

26. *administration* -- This administration has been in office long enough.

27. *absence* -- Absence makes the heart grow fonder and the grades grow lower.

28. *indispensable* -- The indispensable worker could not be replaced.

29. *ridiculous* -- The dress is beautiful but the price is ridiculous.

30. *substantial* -- A substantial down payment is required to buy the house.

ANSWERS AND EXPLANATIONS
FOR MODEL TEST THREE

Computational Facility

1. **(C)**

120	60
OF	100

$120 \times 100 = 12,000$

$12000 \div 60 = \mathbf{200}$

2. **(A)**

$$987$$
$$\underline{135}$$
$$\mathbf{1122}$$

3. **(D)**

$$3768$$
$$\underline{\times \ 547}$$
$$26376$$
$$15072$$
$$\underline{18840}$$
$$\mathbf{206,1096}$$

4. **(B)**

$$98,356$$
$$\underline{- \ 79,398}$$
$$\mathbf{18,958}$$

5. **(B)**

$$5\frac{3}{4} + 7\frac{1}{3} = 5\frac{9}{12} + 7\frac{4}{12} = 12\frac{13}{12} = \mathbf{13\frac{1}{12}}$$

6. **(A)**

$$98,354$$
$$\underline{- \ 97,589}$$
$$\mathbf{765}$$

7. **(B)**

$$\frac{25}{6} \div \frac{34}{5} = \frac{25}{6} \times \frac{5}{34} = \mathbf{\frac{125}{204}}$$

8. **(B)**

$$89,396$$
$$\underline{+ \ 30,105}$$
$$\mathbf{119,501}$$

9. **(C)**

IS	5.8
220	100

$5.8 \times 220 = 1276.0$

$1276 \div 100 = \mathbf{12.76}$

10. **(D)** $\dfrac{8}{11} \times \dfrac{3}{4} = \dfrac{6}{11}$

11. **(A)**

$$
\begin{array}{r}
352 \\
17\overline{)5984} \\
51 \\
\overline{88} \\
85 \\
\overline{34} \\
34 \\
\end{array}
$$

12. **(D)**

$$
\begin{array}{r}
5.600 \\
.084 \\
+\ .150 \\
\hline
\mathbf{5.834} \\
\end{array}
$$

13. **(B)**

64	%
512	100

$64 \times 100 = 6,400$

$6,400 \div 512 = \mathbf{12\dfrac{1}{2}}$

14. **(A)** $15\dfrac{2}{18} - 7\dfrac{15}{18} = 14\dfrac{20}{18} - 7\dfrac{15}{18} = 7\dfrac{\mathbf{5}}{\mathbf{18}}$

15. **(D)**

$$
\begin{array}{r}
16.8 \\
5.2\overline{)87.36} \\
52 \\
\overline{353} \\
312 \\
\overline{416} \\
416 \\
\end{array}
$$

16. **(C)**

$$
\begin{array}{r}
89.300 \\
-17.358 \\
\hline
\mathbf{71.942} \\
\end{array}
$$

17. **(A)**

$$
\begin{array}{r}
3.05 \\
\times\ 9.2 \\
\hline
610 \\
2745 \\
\hline
\mathbf{28.060} \\
\end{array}
$$

18. **(A)**

$$
\begin{array}{r}
156 \\
\times\ 79 \\
\hline
1404 \\
1092 \\
\hline
\mathbf{12,324} \\
\end{array}
$$

19. **(B)**
```
        .86
17)14.62
     136
     102
     102
```

20. **(C)**

IS	35
450	100

$35 \times 450 = 15750$

$15750 \div 100 = \mathbf{157.5}$

Following Directions

1. **(D)**   6. **(B)**   11. **(D)**

2. **(D)**   7. **(C)**   12. **(C)**

3. **(A)**   8. **(C)**   13. **(D)**

4. **(C)**   9. **(A)**   14. **(B)**

5. **(D)**   10. **(A)**   15. **(D)**

Number Groups

1. **(D)** Each number is consecutive ascending. 5432 is different because it is consecutive descending.

2. **(D)** Each number is an arrangement of three 0s and one 1. 1001 is different because there are two 1s.

3. **(B)** All numbers end in an odd number except for 2876 which ends in an even number.

4. **(C)** The first number plus the second number is equal to the third number. 195 is different because 1 + 9 equals 10 not 5.

5. **(D)** The inside numbers are consecutive ascending. 4874 is different because the inside 87 is consecutive descending.

6. **(A)** The sum of the inside numbers is the first number. 9581 is different because the inside sum of 5 + 8 = 13 not 9.

7. **(C)** The first number times the second is equal to the last number. 520 is different because 5 times 2 is equal to 10, not 0.

8. **(C)** The numbers are odd. 4004 is different because it ends in 4, an even number.

9. **(B)** The last three numbers are 543. The first number is odd. 4543 is different because it begins with an even number.

10. **(C)** These numbers have a consecutive difference of 2. 4682 is different because the last number is not 2 more than the previous number 8.

11. **(C)** The first and last pair of numbers and the last pair are the same. 1411 is different because 14 and 11 are not the same.

12. **(C)** 7654 is different because it is the only even number.

13. **(A)** The first pair and the second pair of numbers have a common difference of 15. 1520 is different because the common difference between 15 and 20 is only 5.

14. **(B)** The first number is equal to the sum of the second and third number. 515 is different because 5 + 1 = 6 not 5.

15. **(D)** Each number is an arrangement of the numbers 6, 7, 8, 9. 9685 does not have the number 7.

16. **(A)** The sum of the two outside numbers is equal to the inside pair of numbers. 7134 is different becuase 7 + 4 = 11 not 13.

17. **(D)** 9666 is different because it does not have four of the same number.

18. **(B)** The last three digits repeat. 6224 is different because the last number is 4 instead of repeating 2.

19. **(D)** The first pair of numbers are repeating even numbers. 1100 is different because the first pair 11 is repeating odd.

20. **(C)** The sum of the first two numbers is equal to 9 and the last number is 0. 910 is different becuase the sum of 9 + 1 is 10 not 9.

Spelling

Check spelling list for correct spelling.

1. (B)	6. (D)	11. (C)	16. (D)	21. (D)	26. (C)
2. (D)	7. (C)	12. (A)	17. (D)	22. (B)	27. (B)
3. (B)	8. (A)	13. (C)	18. (C)	23. (C)	28. (C)
4. (A)	9. (B)	14. (D)	19. (B)	24. (A)	29. (C)
5. (C)	10. (A)	15. (A)	20. (B)	25. (C)	30. (D)

MODEL TEST FOUR ANSWER SHEET

COMPUTATIONAL FACILITY

1 Ⓐ Ⓑ Ⓒ Ⓓ   5 Ⓐ Ⓑ Ⓒ Ⓓ   9 Ⓐ Ⓑ Ⓒ Ⓓ   13 Ⓐ Ⓑ Ⓒ Ⓓ   17 Ⓐ Ⓑ Ⓒ Ⓓ
2 Ⓐ Ⓑ Ⓒ Ⓓ   6 Ⓐ Ⓑ Ⓒ Ⓓ   10 Ⓐ Ⓑ Ⓒ Ⓓ   14 Ⓐ Ⓑ Ⓒ Ⓓ   18 Ⓐ Ⓑ Ⓒ Ⓓ
3 Ⓐ Ⓑ Ⓒ Ⓓ   7 Ⓐ Ⓑ Ⓒ Ⓓ   11 Ⓐ Ⓑ Ⓒ Ⓓ   15 Ⓐ Ⓑ Ⓒ Ⓓ   19 Ⓐ Ⓑ Ⓒ Ⓓ
4 Ⓐ Ⓑ Ⓒ Ⓓ   8 Ⓐ Ⓑ Ⓒ Ⓓ   12 Ⓐ Ⓑ Ⓒ Ⓓ   16 Ⓐ Ⓑ Ⓒ Ⓓ   20 Ⓐ Ⓑ Ⓒ Ⓓ

FOLLOWING DIRECTIONS

1 Ⓐ Ⓑ Ⓒ Ⓓ   6 Ⓐ Ⓑ Ⓒ Ⓓ   11 Ⓐ Ⓑ Ⓒ Ⓓ
2 Ⓐ Ⓑ Ⓒ Ⓓ   7 Ⓐ Ⓑ Ⓒ Ⓓ   12 Ⓐ Ⓑ Ⓒ Ⓓ
3 Ⓐ Ⓑ Ⓒ Ⓓ   8 Ⓐ Ⓑ Ⓒ Ⓓ   13 Ⓐ Ⓑ Ⓒ Ⓓ
4 Ⓐ Ⓑ Ⓒ Ⓓ   9 Ⓐ Ⓑ Ⓒ Ⓓ   14 Ⓐ Ⓑ Ⓒ Ⓓ
5 Ⓐ Ⓑ Ⓒ Ⓓ   10 Ⓐ Ⓑ Ⓒ Ⓓ   15 Ⓐ Ⓑ Ⓒ Ⓓ

NUMBER GROUPS

1 Ⓐ Ⓑ Ⓒ Ⓓ   5 Ⓐ Ⓑ Ⓒ Ⓓ   9 Ⓐ Ⓑ Ⓒ Ⓓ   13 Ⓐ Ⓑ Ⓒ Ⓓ   17 Ⓐ Ⓑ Ⓒ Ⓓ
2 Ⓐ Ⓑ Ⓒ Ⓓ   6 Ⓐ Ⓑ Ⓒ Ⓓ   10 Ⓐ Ⓑ Ⓒ Ⓓ   14 Ⓐ Ⓑ Ⓒ Ⓓ   18 Ⓐ Ⓑ Ⓒ Ⓓ
3 Ⓐ Ⓑ Ⓒ Ⓓ   7 Ⓐ Ⓑ Ⓒ Ⓓ   11 Ⓐ Ⓑ Ⓒ Ⓓ   15 Ⓐ Ⓑ Ⓒ Ⓓ   19 Ⓐ Ⓑ Ⓒ Ⓓ
4 Ⓐ Ⓑ Ⓒ Ⓓ   8 Ⓐ Ⓑ Ⓒ Ⓓ   12 Ⓐ Ⓑ Ⓒ Ⓓ   16 Ⓐ Ⓑ Ⓒ Ⓓ   20 Ⓐ Ⓑ Ⓒ Ⓓ

SPELLING

1 Ⓐ Ⓑ Ⓒ Ⓓ   7 Ⓐ Ⓑ Ⓒ Ⓓ   13 Ⓐ Ⓑ Ⓒ Ⓓ   19 Ⓐ Ⓑ Ⓒ Ⓓ   25 Ⓐ Ⓑ Ⓒ Ⓓ
2 Ⓐ Ⓑ Ⓒ Ⓓ   8 Ⓐ Ⓑ Ⓒ Ⓓ   14 Ⓐ Ⓑ Ⓒ Ⓓ   20 Ⓐ Ⓑ Ⓒ Ⓓ   26 Ⓐ Ⓑ Ⓒ Ⓓ
3 Ⓐ Ⓑ Ⓒ Ⓓ   9 Ⓐ Ⓑ Ⓒ Ⓓ   15 Ⓐ Ⓑ Ⓒ Ⓓ   21 Ⓐ Ⓑ Ⓒ Ⓓ   27 Ⓐ Ⓑ Ⓒ Ⓓ
4 Ⓐ Ⓑ Ⓒ Ⓓ   10 Ⓐ Ⓑ Ⓒ Ⓓ   16 Ⓐ Ⓑ Ⓒ Ⓓ   22 Ⓐ Ⓑ Ⓒ Ⓓ   28 Ⓐ Ⓑ Ⓒ Ⓓ
5 Ⓐ Ⓑ Ⓒ Ⓓ   11 Ⓐ Ⓑ Ⓒ Ⓓ   17 Ⓐ Ⓑ Ⓒ Ⓓ   23 Ⓐ Ⓑ Ⓒ Ⓓ   29 Ⓐ Ⓑ Ⓒ Ⓓ
6 Ⓐ Ⓑ Ⓒ Ⓓ   12 Ⓐ Ⓑ Ⓒ Ⓓ   18 Ⓐ Ⓑ Ⓒ Ⓓ   24 Ⓐ Ⓑ Ⓒ Ⓓ   30 Ⓐ Ⓑ Ⓒ Ⓓ

Model Test Four

COMPUTATIONAL FACILITY

Time: 9 Minutes. 20 Questions.

This test measures the ability to do arithmetic problems accurately.

Directions: *Solve each of the following mathematical operations. Mark your answers on the sample answer sheet.*

1. $3\ 5/9 + 4\ 1/6$
   - (A) 132/18
   - (B) 7 13/18
   - (C) 10 39/54
   - (D) None of the Above

2. $28.321 - .89$
   - (A) 27.331
   - (B) 27.431
   - (C) 27.411
   - (D) None of the Above

3. $31,920 \div 912$
   - (A) 35
   - (B) 33
   - (C) 337
   - (D) None of the Above

4. $38 + 97 + 26 + 102$
   - (A) 267
   - (B) 273
   - (C) 264
   - (D) None of the Above

5. $12\ 3/8 - 5\ 4/5$
   - (A) 6 31/40
   - (B) 6 23/40
   - (C) 6 1/5
   - (D) None of the Above

6. 60% of what is 90?

(A) 15
(B) 150
(C) 1.5
(D) None of the Above

7. 356×12

(A) 712
(B) 4282
(C) 3512
(D) None of the Above

8. $9382 - 251$

(A) 9121
(B) 9131
(C) 9031
(D) None of the Above

9. 50% of 110 is what?

(A) 55
(B) 550
(C) 5.5
(D) None of the Above

10. $38,764 - 8025$

(A) 30,739
(B) 30,731
(C) 30,721
(D) None of the Above

11. $22.932 \div 1.82$

(A) .126
(B) .1251
(C) 12.6
(D) 11.47

12. $3\frac{1}{6} \times 18$

(A) 54 1/6
(B) 57
(C) 93
(D) None of the Above

13. $38.617 + 3.4 + 7.80$

(A) 39.722
(B) 48.917
(C) 48.702
(D) None of the Above

14. $2\frac{1}{2} \times 5\frac{1}{4}$

(A) 13 1/5
(B) 10 3/4
(C) 13 1/8
(D) None of the Above

15. 18 is what percent of 30?

(A) 540
(B) 60
(C) 16.66
(D) None of the Above

16. 2101 - 835

(A) 1267
(B) 266
(C) 1266
(D) None of the Above

17. 81.2×30.1

(A) 2444.12
(B) 2544.12
(C) 2644.12
(D) None of the Above

18. 387×21

(A) 8141
(B) 8107
(C) 8207
(D) None of the Above

19. What percent of 100 is 45?

(A) 20
(B) 45
(C) .45
(D) None of the Above

20. $18 \div 6\frac{2}{7}$

(A) 2 38/44
(B) 2 19/22
(C) 2 1/2
(D) None of the Above

FOLLOWING DIRECTIONS

Time: 10 Minutes. 15 Questions.

This test measures your ability to follow both written and oral instructions.

<u>Directions</u>: *Use the table below to follow the written and oral directions. Mark your answers on the sample answer sheet.*

<u>To the Test Assistant</u>: *Turn to page 179 for the oral instructions. If you do not have someone to read the oral directions for you, record them yourself and play them back when you begin the exam.*

	Column				
	A	B	C	D	E
Row 1	1	M	NN	M	4
Row 2	3	2	N	2	MM
Row 3	1	P	3	PP	2
Row 4	P	2	NN	N	3
Row 5	1	MM	3	2	5

1. What number or letter is on Row 3 Column E?

   (A) MM   (B) 3   (C) 2   (D) 5

2. Mark the number that does not appear in the table.

   (A) 3   (B) 2   (C) 6   (D) 5

3. What number is in the middle of the table?

   (A) 1   (B) 2   (C) 3   (D) 4

4. Which number is first in more than one row?

   (A) 1   (B) 3   (C) 4   (D) 5

5. How many times does the number 1 appear in the table?

   (A) 2   (B) 3   (C) 4   (D) 5

6. Which number or letter appears twice in Column D?

    (A) 1   (B) 2   (C) N   (D) 4

7. Which column contains only one letter?

    (A) A   (B) 2   (C) 5   (D) E

8. What letter or number would be below PP if Row 3 were reversed?

    (A) P   (B) 2   (C) 3   (D) 4

9. Find the letter or number on Column D Row 3.

    (A) P   (B) PP   (C) M   (D) 1

10. Locate the column that contains three different letters and mark the correct response.

    (A) A   (B) B   (C) C   (D) D

11. How many numbers are in the table?

    (A) 12   (B) 13   (C) 14   (D) 15

12. What is the number or letter in Row 3 that is just below the letter N?

    (A) 1   (B) 2   (C) 3   (D) P

13. What letter or number is two spaces to the right of the letter that is just above the letter that is three spaces to the left of the last position in Row 2?

    (A) M   (B) 4   (C) PP   (D) 2

14. If Row 1 was reversed, and Row 5 was reversed, which Column would contain the most M's?

    (A) B   (B) C   (C) D   (D) E

15. How many times does the number 3 appear in the table?

    (A) 2   (B) 3   (C) 4   (D) 5

NUMBER GROUPS

Time: 7 Minutes. 20 Questions.

This is a test of your ability to see how groups of numbers are alike or different.

Directions: *Each problem has four groups of numbers; three of the number groups have something in common. Darken the choice on your sample answer sheet that corresponds to the one group that is different from the other three.*

1.	(A) 4011	(B) 5011	(C) 3011	(D) 7011
2.	(A) 6633	(B) 4422	(C) 8844	(D) 5522
3.	(A) 5142	(B) 6005	(C) 4331	(D) 3512
4.	(A) 1135	(B) 1325	(C) 5311	(D) 3151
5.	(A) 3456	(B) 1234	(C) 7654	(D) 2345
6.	(A) 8324	(B) 7642	(C) 5420	(D) 6532
7.	(A) 1221	(B) 5445	(C) 7667	(D) 3223
8.	(A) 9753	(B) 7531	(C) 8642	(D) 6432
9.	(A) 3814	(B) 1346	(C) 4813	(D) 8431
10.	(A) 1234	(B) 5311	(C) 3304	(D) 5431
11.	(A) 2615	(B) 2616	(C) 2716	(D) 2617
12.	(A) 6789	(B) 8765	(C) 3456	(D) 1234
13.	(A) 333	(B) 555	(C) 888	(D) 777
14.	(A) 515	(B) 325	(C) 818	(D) 900
15.	(A) 835	(B) 624	(C) 945	(D) 724
16.	(A) 7124	(B) 6513	(C) 9006	(D) 8205
17.	(A) 302	(B) 807	(C) 506	(D) 403
18.	(A) 2714	(B) 3515	(C) 4104	(D) 6213
19.	(A) 1001	(B) 1011	(C) 1100	(D) 1010
20.	(A) 6070	(B) 5060	(C) 3020	(D) 8090

SPELLING

Time: 12 Minutes. 30 Questions.

This test measures your ability to spell words correctly.

Directions: For each question a test assistant will pronounce a word to be spelled and then use it in a sentence. On your answer sheet, mark the letter series from the answer choices that is contained in the correct spelling of the word. If you do not have someone to read the words, record them yourself and play them back when you begin the test.

To the Test Assistant: Turn to pages 179-180 for the spelling list and corresponding sentences.

1. The word you have just spelled contains which of the following series of letters?

   (A) accomo   (B) ccomm   (C) acomm   (D) acomo

2. The word you have just spelled contains which of the following series of letters?

   (A) akwi   (B) acqui   (C) aqui   (D) akqui

3. The word you have just spelled contains which of the following series of letters?

   (A) aprop   (B) eprop   (C) apropp   (D) approp

4. The word you have just spelled contains which of the following series of letters?

   (A) nize   (B) nise   (C) mize   (D) nice

5. The word you have just spelled contains which of the following series of letters?

   (A) ascess   (B) assess   (C) asces   (D) asess

6. The word you have just spelled contains which of the following series of letters?

   (A) soff   (B) sof   (C) scoph   (D) soph

7. The word you have just spelled contains which of the following series of letters?

   (A) eous   (B) ious   (C) uous   (D) eios

8. The word you have just spelled contains which of the following series of letters?

   (A) nis   (B) inis   (C) nous   (D) niss

9. The word you have just spelled contains which of the following series of letters?

(A) scid   (B) ncid   (C) nced   (D) ccid

10. The word you have just spelled contains which of the following series of letters?

(A) shient   (B) sient   (C) scient   (D) sheient

11. The word you have just spelled contains which of the following series of letters?

(A) reelly   (B) reely   (C) realy   (D) reall

12. The word you have just spelled contains which of the following series of letters?

(A) contem   (B) contum   (C) contom   (D) contim

13. The word you have just spelled contains which of the following series of letters?

(A) corug   (B) corrug   (C) corog   (D) corrag

14. The word you have just spelled contains which of the following series of letters?

(A) sern   (B) ssern   (C) scern   (D) scurn

15. The word you have just spelled contains which of the following series of letters?

(A) expid   (B) ecxpid   (C) eksped   (D) exped

16. The word you have just spelled contains which of the following series of letters?

(A) birse   (B) burce   (C) burse   (D) birss

17. The word you have just spelled contains which of the following series of letters?

(A) cid   (B) ced   (C) sed   (D) sid

18. The word you have just spelled contains which of the following series of letters?

(A) pal   (B) ple   (C) pple   (D) pall

19. The word you have just spelled contains which of the following series of letters?

(A) rred   (B) rrd   (C) redd   (D) rd

20. The word you have just spelled contains which of the following series of letters?

(A) rrate   (B) rait   (C) rate   (D) rayt

21. The word you have just spelled contains which of the following series of letters?

    (A) ledg   (B) lidg   (C) legg   (D) leg

22. The word you have just spelled contains which of the following series of letters?

    (A) attive   (B) ative   (C) otive   (D) itive

23. The word you have just spelled contains which of the following series of letters?

    (A) misel   (B) misil   (C) miscel   (D) missel

24. The word you have just spelled contains which of the following series of letters?

    (A) missp   (B) misp   (C) mispp   (D) misspp

25. The word you have just spelled contains which of the following series of letters?

    (A) perf   (B) pirf   (C) perph   (D) pirff

26. The word you have just spelled contains which of the following series of letters?

    (A) able   (B) abel   (C) ible   (D) abull

27. The word you have just spelled contains which of the following series of letters?

    (A) mus   (B) miss   (C) mous   (D) maus

28. The word you have just spelled contains which of the following series of letters?

    (A) holy   (B) holle   (C) wholey   (D) wholl

29. The word you have just spelled contains which of the following series of letters?

    (A) ocure   (B) occure   (C) ocurr   (D) occurr

30. The word you have just spelled contains which of the following series of letters?

    (A) veeran   (B) presev   (C) rence   (D) persev

STOP   End of Test

For the Test Assistant

Oral Instructions

Directions: Wait 30 seconds after the test begins then read each question at one minute intervals. Do not repeat any questions. Stop the test at 10 minutes.

1.   If you marked answer C for question number 2, change your answer to B.

2.   If you marked B for question number 3, change your answer to D.

3.   Use Column C instead of Column D to answer question 6. Change your answer if necessary.

4.   Change Row 3 to Row 4 in question 1, change your answer if necessary.

5.   Reverse Column D for question 9, change your answer if necessary.

6.   If you answered B in question number 10 change it to C.

7.   If you changed your answer to B in question number 2, change it now to A.

8.   If you changed your answer in question 6, change it back so that it answers the original question asked.

9.   Change Row 2 to Row 4 in question number 13. Change your answer if necessary.

10.   If you answered C for question number 13, change it to B.

Spelling Words and Sentences

Directions: Read each word and the sentence using that word. Pause 17 seconds before reading the next word to allow the test taker to answer the question. Do not repeat any word or sentence.

1. *accommodate* -- The hotel can accommodate groups of every size.

2. *acquisition* -- That sports car is his latest acquisition.

3. *appropriation* -- Congress may vote to increase the appropriation for space exploration.

4. *recognize* -- I recognize your uncle in the crowd.

5. *assessable* -- The home would not be assessable until the real estate agent could research the sales of homes in the neighborhood.

6. *sophisticated* -- You look very sophisticated in your tuxedo.

7. *simultaneous* -- Simultaneous translations enabled the speaker's words to be carried to listeners across the world.

8. *bituminous* -- Bituminous coal produces a considerable amount of soot.

9. *coincidence* -- They arrived at the same time by coincidence.

10. *conscientious* -- They were conscientious about watering the plants.

11. *really* -- I really don't understand her motives.

12. *contemplating* -- We are contemplating selling our house.

13. *corrugated* -- Corrugated cardboard makes an excellent packaging material.

14. *discernible* -- The road sign was barely discernible in the distance.

15. *expedite* -- Since you are in a hurry, I will expedite your request.

16. *reimburse* -- The company will reimburse your expenses.

17. *precedence* -- Emergency calls take precedence over routine ones.

18. *principal* -- The principal reason he moved to the city was to find employment.

19. *inferred* -- Her motive could not be inferred by the expression on her face.

20. *deteriorate* -- Exposure to the elements will cause paint to deteriorate.

21. *legitimate* -- They are the legitimate heirs to the fortune.

22. *lucrative* -- The company pursued the lucrative contract.

23. *miscellaneous* -- Do you think the IRS will notice if my miscellaneous deductions exceed my income?

24. *misspelled* -- I think I misspelled the word misspelled.

25. *superflous* -- The excess chrome on this car is superflous.

26. *tangible* -- My house is my only tangible asset.

27. *unanimous* -- They won by the unanimous decision of all the judges.

28. *wholly* -- The shop was wholly owned by the parent company.

29. *occurred* -- World War II occurred before I was born.

30. *perseverance* -- Perseverance will get you through this test.

ANSWERS AND EXPLANATIONS
FOR MODEL TEST FOUR

Computational Facility

1. **(B)** $3\dfrac{10}{18} + 4\dfrac{3}{18} = 7\dfrac{13}{18}$

2. **(B)**
$$\begin{array}{r} 28.321 \\ -\ \ .890 \\ \hline \mathbf{27.431} \end{array}$$

3. **(A)**
$$\begin{array}{r} 35 \\ 912)\overline{31920} \\ \underline{2736} \\ 4560 \\ \underline{4560} \end{array}$$

4. **(D)**
$$\begin{array}{r} 38 \\ 97 \\ 26 \\ +102 \\ \hline \mathbf{263} \end{array}$$

5. **(B)** $12\dfrac{15}{40} - 5\dfrac{32}{40} = 11\dfrac{55}{40} - 5\dfrac{32}{40} = \mathbf{6\dfrac{23}{40}}$

6. **(B)**

90	60
OF	100

$90 \times 100 = 9,000$

$9,000 \div 60 = \mathbf{150}$

7. **(D)**
$$\begin{array}{r} 356 \\ \times\ 12 \\ \hline 712 \\ 356 \\ \hline \mathbf{4272} \end{array}$$

8. **(B)**
$$\begin{array}{r} 9382 \\ -251 \\ \hline \mathbf{9,131} \end{array}$$

9. **(A)**

IS	50
110	100

$50 \times 110 = 5500$

$5500 \div 100 = \mathbf{55}$

10. **(A)** 38,764
       - 8,025
      30,739

11. **(C)**

$$
\begin{array}{r}
\underline{\mathbf{12.6}} \\
182)\overline{2293.2} \\
\underline{182} \\
473 \\
\underline{364} \\
1092 \\
\underline{1092}
\end{array}
$$

12. **(B)** $\dfrac{19}{6} \times \dfrac{18}{1} = \dfrac{57}{1} = \mathbf{57}$

13. **(D)** 38.617
     3.400
   + 7.800
   49.817

14. **(C)** $\dfrac{5}{2} \times \dfrac{21}{4} = \dfrac{105}{8} = \mathbf{13\dfrac{1}{8}}$

15. **(B)**

18	%
30	100

$18 \times 100 = 1800$
$1800 \div 30 = \mathbf{60}$

16. **(C)** 2101
   - 835
   1266

17. **(A)**   81.2
   x 30.1
     812
     000
   2436
   2444.12

18. **(D)** 387
   x 21
   387
   774
   8127

19. **(B)**

45	%
100	100

$45 \times 100 = 4500$
$4500 \div 100 = \mathbf{45}$

20. **(B)** $\dfrac{18}{1} \div \dfrac{44}{7} = \dfrac{18}{1} \times \dfrac{7}{44} = \dfrac{63}{22} = 2\dfrac{19}{22}$

Following Directions

1. **(B)**	6. **(B)**	11. **(C)**
2. **(A)**	7. **(A)**	12. **(C)**
3. **(C)**	8. **(B)**	13. **(B)**
4. **(A)**	9. **(B)**	14. **(C)**
5. **(B)**	10. **(D)**	15. **(C)**

Number Groups

1. **(A)**   The first number in number sequence (A) is an even number. Choices (B), (C), and (D) all begin with an odd number.

2. **(D)**   In the first three choices, the last two digits times 2 is equal to the first two digits. 5522 is not correct because 22 x 2 = 44, not 55.

3. **(A)**   The sum of all digits in each number is 11. 5142 is different because the sum of 5 + 1 + 4 + 2 = 12 not 11.

4. **(B)**   Each number is a combination of the numbers 1, 1, 3, 5. 1325 has the number 2 which is not a part of this combination.

5. **(C)**   Each number is consecutive ascending. 7654 is consecutive descending.

6. **(D)**   The first number times the second number equals the last pair of numbers. 6532 is different because 6 times 5 equals 30 not 32.

7. **(A)**   The outside digits are 1 more than the inside digits. 1221 is different because the outside digits are one less than the inside digits.

8. **(D)**   Each number has a consecutive difference of 2. 6432 is different because to follow the pattern the numbers should be 6420.

9. **(B)**   These are combinations of the numbers 1, 3, 4, 8. 1346 is different because it has a 6.

10. **(D)** The sum of all the digits in each number is 10. The sum of the digits in 5431 is 13.

11. **(C)** All the numbers begin with 261 except for 2716.

12. **(B)** Each number is consecutive ascending. 8765 is consecutive descending.

13. **(C)** All numbers are odd except 888 which is even.

14. **(B)** The product of first pair of digits is the last number. 325 is different because 3 x 2 = 6 not 5.

15. **(D)** The sum of the last pair of digits is the first number. 724 is different because 2 + 4 = 6 not 7.

16. **(A)** The sum of all the digits in each number is 15. The sum of the digits in 7124 is 14.

17. **(C)** The outside digits are consecutive descending. 506 is different because the outside digits are consecutive ascending.

18. **(D)** The product of the first pair of digits is equal to the last pair of digits in each number. In 6213, the product of 6 x 2 = 12 not 13.

19. **(B)** Each number is a different arrangement of 1,1,0,0. 1011 has an extra 1.

20. **(C)** The first and third digit are consecutive ascending. 3020 has consecutive descending digits.

Spelling

1. **(B)**	6. **(D)**	11. **(D)**	16. **(C)**	21. **(D)**	26. **(C)**
2. **(B)**	7. **(A)**	12. **(A)**	17. **(B)**	22. **(B)**	27. **(C)**
3. **(D)**	8. **(C)**	13. **(B)**	18. **(A)**	23. **(C)**	28. **(D)**
4. **(A)**	9. **(B)**	14. **(C)**	19. **(A)**	24. **(A)**	29. **(D)**
5. **(B)**	10. **(C)**	15. **(D)**	20. **(C)**	25. **(A)**	30. **(D)**

MODEL TEST FIVE ANSWER SHEET

COMPUTATIONAL FACILITY

1 Ⓐ Ⓑ Ⓒ Ⓓ   5 Ⓐ Ⓑ Ⓒ Ⓓ   9 Ⓐ Ⓑ Ⓒ Ⓓ   13 Ⓐ Ⓑ Ⓒ Ⓓ   17 Ⓐ Ⓑ Ⓒ Ⓓ
2 Ⓐ Ⓑ Ⓒ Ⓓ   6 Ⓐ Ⓑ Ⓒ Ⓓ   10 Ⓐ Ⓑ Ⓒ Ⓓ   14 Ⓐ Ⓑ Ⓒ Ⓓ   18 Ⓐ Ⓑ Ⓒ Ⓓ
3 Ⓐ Ⓑ Ⓒ Ⓓ   7 Ⓐ Ⓑ Ⓒ Ⓓ   11 Ⓐ Ⓑ Ⓒ Ⓓ   15 Ⓐ Ⓑ Ⓒ Ⓓ   19 Ⓐ Ⓑ Ⓒ Ⓓ
4 Ⓐ Ⓑ Ⓒ Ⓓ   8 Ⓐ Ⓑ Ⓒ Ⓓ   12 Ⓐ Ⓑ Ⓒ Ⓓ   16 Ⓐ Ⓑ Ⓒ Ⓓ   20 Ⓐ Ⓑ Ⓒ Ⓓ

FOLLOWING DIRECTIONS

1 Ⓐ Ⓑ Ⓒ Ⓓ   6 Ⓐ Ⓑ Ⓒ Ⓓ   11 Ⓐ Ⓑ Ⓒ Ⓓ
2 Ⓐ Ⓑ Ⓒ Ⓓ   7 Ⓐ Ⓑ Ⓒ Ⓓ   12 Ⓐ Ⓑ Ⓒ Ⓓ
3 Ⓐ Ⓑ Ⓒ Ⓓ   8 Ⓐ Ⓑ Ⓒ Ⓓ   13 Ⓐ Ⓑ Ⓒ Ⓓ
4 Ⓐ Ⓑ Ⓒ Ⓓ   9 Ⓐ Ⓑ Ⓒ Ⓓ   14 Ⓐ Ⓑ Ⓒ Ⓓ
5 Ⓐ Ⓑ Ⓒ Ⓓ   10 Ⓐ Ⓑ Ⓒ Ⓓ   15 Ⓐ Ⓑ Ⓒ Ⓓ

NUMBER GROUPS

1 Ⓐ Ⓑ Ⓒ Ⓓ   5 Ⓐ Ⓑ Ⓒ Ⓓ   9 Ⓐ Ⓑ Ⓒ Ⓓ   13 Ⓐ Ⓑ Ⓒ Ⓓ   17 Ⓐ Ⓑ Ⓒ Ⓓ
2 Ⓐ Ⓑ Ⓒ Ⓓ   6 Ⓐ Ⓑ Ⓒ Ⓓ   10 Ⓐ Ⓑ Ⓒ Ⓓ   14 Ⓐ Ⓑ Ⓒ Ⓓ   18 Ⓐ Ⓑ Ⓒ Ⓓ
3 Ⓐ Ⓑ Ⓒ Ⓓ   7 Ⓐ Ⓑ Ⓒ Ⓓ   11 Ⓐ Ⓑ Ⓒ Ⓓ   15 Ⓐ Ⓑ Ⓒ Ⓓ   19 Ⓐ Ⓑ Ⓒ Ⓓ
4 Ⓐ Ⓑ Ⓒ Ⓓ   8 Ⓐ Ⓑ Ⓒ Ⓓ   12 Ⓐ Ⓑ Ⓒ Ⓓ   16 Ⓐ Ⓑ Ⓒ Ⓓ   20 Ⓐ Ⓑ Ⓒ Ⓓ

SPELLING

1 Ⓐ Ⓑ Ⓒ Ⓓ   7 Ⓐ Ⓑ Ⓒ Ⓓ   13 Ⓐ Ⓑ Ⓒ Ⓓ   19 Ⓐ Ⓑ Ⓒ Ⓓ   25 Ⓐ Ⓑ Ⓒ Ⓓ
2 Ⓐ Ⓑ Ⓒ Ⓓ   8 Ⓐ Ⓑ Ⓒ Ⓓ   14 Ⓐ Ⓑ Ⓒ Ⓓ   20 Ⓐ Ⓑ Ⓒ Ⓓ   26 Ⓐ Ⓑ Ⓒ Ⓓ
3 Ⓐ Ⓑ Ⓒ Ⓓ   9 Ⓐ Ⓑ Ⓒ Ⓓ   15 Ⓐ Ⓑ Ⓒ Ⓓ   21 Ⓐ Ⓑ Ⓒ Ⓓ   27 Ⓐ Ⓑ Ⓒ Ⓓ
4 Ⓐ Ⓑ Ⓒ Ⓓ   10 Ⓐ Ⓑ Ⓒ Ⓓ   16 Ⓐ Ⓑ Ⓒ Ⓓ   22 Ⓐ Ⓑ Ⓒ Ⓓ   28 Ⓐ Ⓑ Ⓒ Ⓓ
5 Ⓐ Ⓑ Ⓒ Ⓓ   11 Ⓐ Ⓑ Ⓒ Ⓓ   17 Ⓐ Ⓑ Ⓒ Ⓓ   23 Ⓐ Ⓑ Ⓒ Ⓓ   29 Ⓐ Ⓑ Ⓒ Ⓓ
6 Ⓐ Ⓑ Ⓒ Ⓓ   12 Ⓐ Ⓑ Ⓒ Ⓓ   18 Ⓐ Ⓑ Ⓒ Ⓓ   24 Ⓐ Ⓑ Ⓒ Ⓓ   30 Ⓐ Ⓑ Ⓒ Ⓓ

Model Test Five

COMPUTATIONAL FACILITY

Time: 9 Minutes. 20 Questions.

This test measures the ability to do arithmetic problems accurately.

Directions: _Solve each of the following mathematical operations. Mark your answers on the sample answer sheet._

1. $103 + 26 + 15 + 48 + 25$
   - (A) 218
   - (B) 216
   - (C) 217
   - (D) None of the Above

2. $1070 - 959$
   - (A) 121
   - (B) 129
   - (C) 119
   - (D) None of the Above

3. $1886 \div 23$
   - (A) 122
   - (B) 75
   - (C) 82
   - (D) None of the Above

4. 2398×52
   - (A) 120,696
   - (B) 124,696
   - (C) 124,966
   - (D) None of the Above

5. $\dfrac{8}{27} \times \dfrac{9}{16}$
   - (A) 1/6
   - (B) 1/4
   - (C) 1/3
   - (D) None of the Above

187

6. $\dfrac{17}{30} - \dfrac{9}{20}$

(A) 4/5
(B) 2/5
(C) 7/60
(D) none of the Above

7. $8\dfrac{1}{5} \times 2$

(A) 18
(B) 16 2/5
(C) 16 1/5
(D) None of the Above

8. What is 5% of 18?

(A) 90
(B) 9
(C) .09
(D) None of the Above

9. $1\dfrac{1}{3} \div \dfrac{8}{9}$

(A) 1 1/2
(B) 8/27
(C) 1 5/9
(D) None of the Above

10. 3.3 + .46 + 88

(A) 1.67
(B) 88.79
(C) 91.76
(D) None of the Above

11. 8.6 × 2.1

(A) 16.6
(B) 16.06
(C) 180.6
(D) 18.06

12. .07 × .03

(A) .21
(B) .0021
(C) 2.1
(D) .021

13. 38.15 - 21.7

(A) 16.45
(B) 35.98
(C) 17.8
(D) 17.45

14. What is 60% of 95?

(A) 158
(B) 57
(C) 15.8
(D) 570

15. $388 \div 0.4$

(A) 103
(B) 97
(C) 10.3
(D) 970

16. 16.17 is what percent of 46.2?

(A) 35
(B) 2.9
(C) 2900
(D) 29

17. 102×98

(A) 996
(B) 9916
(C) 9996
(D) None of the Above

18. $2.31 \div .21$

(A) 1.1
(B) 1.01
(C) .11
(D) 11

19. 63.2 is 40% of what number?

(A) 252.8
(B) 15.8
(C) 158
(D) 25.28

20. What is 0.3% of 103?

(A) 34.3
(B) 30.9
(C) .309
(D) 3.09

FOLLOWING DIRECTIONS

Time: 10 Minutes. 15 Questions.

This test measures your ability to follow both written and oral instructions.

Directions: Use the table below to follow the written and oral directions. Mark your answers on the sample answer sheet.

To The Test Assistant: Turn to page 197 for the oral instructions. If you do not have someone to read the oral directions for you, record them yourself and play them back when you begin the exam.

	Column				
	1	2	3	4	5
Row 1	X	Y	Z	W	Q
Row 2	2	3	4	7	8
Row 3	Y	W	Z	X	Q
Row 4	Z	5	X	2	Y
Row 5	8	7	5	3	2
Row 6	X	Y	Z	W	Q

1. What number is below X in Row 4 Column 3?

   (A) 8   (B) 3   (C) 2   (D) 5

2. What letter is to the left of Z in Row 3 Column 3?

   (A) W   (B) X   (C) Y   (D) Z

3. What is the sum of the numbers in Column 2?

   (A) 15   (B) 24   (C) 23   (D) 17

4. Which letter is not in Row 4?

   (A) W   (B) X   (C) Y   (D) Z

5. Reverse Row 2. What number is in Row 2 Column 5?

   (A) 8   (B) 2   (C) 3   (D) 7

6. What letter or number is 2 spaces below the number in Column 4 Row 2?

    (A) Y   (B) X   (C) W   (D) 2

7. Which number is not in the table?

    (A) 5   (B) 6   (C) 7   (D) 8

8. What is the sum of the numbers in Row 5?

    (A) 24   (B) 15   (C) 25   (D) 30

9. Reverse Column 2 and Column 4. What is now to the left of Z in Row 3 Column 3?

    (A) 3   (B) 2   (C) 5   (D) 7

10. What letter is to the left of the letter four spaces below the number in
    Column 5 Row 2?

    (A) X   (B) Y   (C) 2   (D) W

11. Reverse Row 3 and Row 6. What letter is two spaces above the space that is above
    the space to the left of the letter in Row 6 Column 4?

    (A) W   (B) X   (C) Y   (D) Z

12. In Column 4 what is just below the letter X?

    (A) Y   (B) 5   (C) 2   (D) 7

13. How many times does the letter X appear in the table?

    (A) 3   (B) 4   (C) 5   (D) 6

14. Add the numbers in Row 2. Subtract from this number the sum of the numbers in
    Column 4. What number is twice this sum?

    (A) 6   (B) 24   (C) 28   (D) 12

15. What is below the letter to the right of the letter X in Column 3?

    (A) 1   (B) 2   (C) 3   (D) 4

NUMBER GROUPS

Time: 7 Minutes. 20 Questions.

This is a test of your ability to see how groups of numbers are alike or different.

Directions: Each problem has four groups of numbers; three of the number groups have something in common. Darken the choice on your sample answer sheet that corresponds to the one group that is different from the other three.

1.	(A) 8888	(B) 8882	(C) 8885	(D) 8886
2.	(A) 8765	(B) 7654	(C) 4321	(D) 6789
3.	(A) 6126	(B) 8145	(C) 7103	(D) 9178
4.	(A) 2538	(B) 2546	(C) 2523	(D) 2567
5.	(A) 1002	(B) 3004	(C) 5006	(D) 6007
6.	(A) 2202	(B) 3206	(C) 4208	(D) 1202
7.	(A) 7512	(B) 8614	(C) 9514	(D) 8716
8.	(A) 0011	(B) 2200	(C) 3300	(D) 5500
9.	(A) 3033	(B) 3330	(C) 3030	(D) 0333
10.	(A) 1444	(B) 7777	(C) 6666	(D) 5555
11.	(A) 3782	(B) 2387	(C) 8732	(D) 3875
12.	(A) 8897	(B) 7675	(C) 5453	(D) 3231
13.	(A) 7763	(B) 3320	(C) 5541	(D) 9985
14.	(A) 2468	(B) 8642	(C) 2648	(D) 4680
15.	(A) 3366	(B) 2244	(C) 1123	(D) 4488
16.	(A) 2020	(B) 8080	(C) 6060	(D) 0404
17.	(A) 8070	(B) 4191	(C) 5262	(D) 3427
18.	(A) 4554	(B) 5665	(C) 3223	(D) 8998
19.	(A) 1000	(B) 4000	(C) 3000	(D) 5000
20.	(A) 6422	(B) 5533	(C) 8244	(D) 4755

SPELLING

Time: 12 Minutes. 30 Questions.

This test measures your ability to spell words correctly.

<u>Directions</u>: *For each question a test assistant will pronounce a word to be spelled and then use it in a sentence. On your answer sheet, mark the letter series from the answer choices that is contained in the correct spelling of the word. If you do not have someone to read the words, record them yourself and play them back when you begin the test.*

<u>To the Test Assistant</u>: *Turn to pages 197-198 for the spelling list and corresponding sentences.*

1. The word you have just spelled contains which of the following series of letters?

    (A) cely   (B) elly   (C) cly   (D) sely

2. The word you have just spelled contains which of the following series of letters?

    (A) deck   (B) dicr   (C) decr   (D) epet

3. The word you have just spelled contains which of the following series of letters?

    A) ecco   (B) ecor   (C) icor   (D) ikor

4. The word you have just spelled contains which of the following series of letters?

    (A) nnow   (B) anow   (C) anno   (D) anou

5. The word you have just spelled contains which of the following series of letters?

    (A) cism   (B) sism   (C) cizm   (D) isem

6. The word you have just spelled contains which of the following series of letters?

    (A) minot   (B) menut   (C) minut   (D) minnu

7. The word you have just spelled contains which of the following series of letters?

    (A) ogme   (B) augm   (C) augh   (D) awgm

8. The word you have just spelled contains which of the following series of letters?

    (A) niess   (B) naess   (C) nnass   (D) naiss

9. The word you have just spelled contains which of the following series of letters?

    (A) osal   (B) puru   (C) usel   (D) usal

10. The word you have just spelled contains which of the following series of letters?

    (A) phern   (B) phren   (C) phana   (D) phirn

11. The word you have just spelled contains which of the following series of letters?

    (A) preity   (B) priaty   (C) prioty   (D) priety

12. The word you have just spelled contains which of the following series of letters?

    (A) promo   (B) promm   (C) premo   (D) pramo

13. The word you have just spelled contains which of the following series of letters?

    (A) enus   (B) yous   (C) ious   (D) nius

14. The word you have just spelled contains which of the following series of letters?

    (A) dense   (B) dance   (C) dunce   (D) danse

15. The word you have just spelled contains which of the following series of letters?

    (A) safic   (B) suffic   (C) sufic   (D) saffi

16. The word you have just spelled contains which of the following series of letters?

    (A) cence   (B) cense   (C) cinse   (D) cience

17. The word you have just spelled contains which of the following series of letters?

    (A) Teus   (B) Tous   (C) Tusd   (D) Tues

18. The word you have just spelled contains which of the following series of letters?

    (A) gence   (B) jense   (C) gense   (D) gince

19. The word you have just spelled contains which of the following series of letters?

    (A) sharl   (B) scharl   (C) sharr   (D) charl

20. The word you have just spelled contains which of the following series of letters?

    (A) vers   (B) verc   (C) virs   (D) virz

21. The word you have just spelled contains which of the following series of letters?

   (A) itie   (B) city   (C) itty   (D) sity

22. The word you have just spelled contains which of the following series of letters?

   (A) vaci   (B) veci   (C) cini   (D) ceni

23. The word you have just spelled contains which of the following series of letters?

   (A) llick   (B) illic   (C) ilick   (D) lliki

24. The word you have just spelled contains which of the following series of letters?

   (A) dint   (B) dent   (C) pind   (D) dape

25. The word you have just spelled contains which of the following series of letters?

   (A) must   (B) ashe   (C) tash   (D) ache

26. The word you have just spelled contains which of the following series of letters?

   (A) exac   (B) ecut   (C) egse   (D) eckx

27. The word you have just spelled contains which of the following series of letters?

   (A) mini   (B) meni   (C) senc   (D) nise

28. The word you have just spelled contains which of the following series of letters?

   (A) lete   (B) cule   (C) late   (D) tick

29. Thc word you have just spelled contains which of the following series of letters?

   (A) aning   (B) skan   (C) nning   (D) neng

30. The word you have just spelled contains which of the following series of letters?

   (A) fisi   (B) phis   (C) sick   (D) ique

| STOP | End of Test |

For the Test Assistant

Oral Instructions

Directions: *Wait 30 seconds after the test begins then read each question at one minute intervals. Do not repeat any questions. Stop the test at 10 minutes.*

1. If you marked A for question 2 change it to B.

2. If you marked C for question 3 change it to D.

3. If you answered C in question 1, change it to D.

4. Use Column 3 instead of Column 4 to answer question 6. Change your answer if necessary.

5. If you answered B to question 7 change it to A.

6. Change the letter X to letter Z in question 13. Change your answer if necessary.

7. If you answered B to question 8, change it to C.

8. If you changed your answer in question 7, change it now so that it answers the original question.

9. Change the word below to above in question 12 and answer accordingly.

10. If you changed your answer to B in question 2 change it to C.

Spelling Words and Sentences

Directions: *Read each word and the sentence using that word. Pause 17 seconds before reading the next word to allow the test taker to answer the question. Do not repeat any word or sentence.*

1. *scarcely* -- The picnic had scarcely begun, when it began to rain.

2. *decrepit* -- He drives the most decrepit car in the city.

3. *record* -- She broke the record for the 100 yard dash.

4. *announce* -- Please announce my presence to your parents.

5. *fanaticism* -- Excessive zeal for a cause may degenerate into fanaticism.

6. *diminutive* -- Napoleon was diminutive in size but large in ambition.

7. *augmented* -- They augmented their salary by working overtime.

8. *reconnaissance* -- The reconnaissance flight pinpointed the position of the enemy.

9. *perusal* -- He only had time for a quick perusal of his mail.

10. *paraphernalia* -- Backpack, maps, ropes, and compasses are some of the paraphernalia that the hiker collected over time.

11. *propriety* -- No matter how provoked, she maintained her sense of propriety.

12. *promotion* -- Diligent work will lead to a promotion.

13. *ingenious* -- Her ingenious solution to the problem was recognized by her co-workers.

14. *abundance* -- America possesses an abundance of national resources.

15. *sufficiently* -- She was sufficiently impressed by his work to offer him the job.

16. *reticence* -- The movie star responded to personal questions with reticence.

17. *Tuesday* -- Is it Tuesday's child who is fair of face?

18. *intelligence* -- Intelligence is the capacity to acquire and apply knowledge.

19. *charlatan* -- The fortune teller was exposed as a charlatan.

20. *anniversary* -- Tomorrow marks the 3rd anniversary of their marriage.

21. *publicity* -- Politicians seek publicity when running for election.

22. *vicinity* -- We live in the vicinity of the park.

23. *rollicking* -- I had a rollicking good time at the party.

24. *dependent* -- The past is not dependent on us for its existence.

25. *moustache* -- He grew a moustache to make him appear older.

26. *executive* -- We reserved the executive suites.

27. *reminiscence* -- The reminiscence of happier times filled his thoughts.

28. *articulate* -- Articulate speech distinquishes the lower animals.

29. *scanning* -- The forest rangers are scanning the horizon for signs of smoke.

30. *physique* -- He has the physique of an olympic swimmer.

ANSWERS AND EXPLANATIONS
FOR MODEL TEST FIVE

Computational Facility

1. **(C)**   Add in pairs $103 + 26 = 129$. $15 + 48 + 25 = 88$. The total is **217**.

2. **(D)**

$$\begin{array}{r} 1070 \\ -959 \\ \hline \mathbf{111} \end{array}$$

3. **(C)**

$$\begin{array}{r} 82 \\ 23)\overline{1886} \\ \underline{184} \\ 46 \\ \underline{46} \end{array}$$

4. **(B)**

$$\begin{array}{r} 2398 \\ \times 52 \\ \hline 4796 \\ \underline{11990} \\ \mathbf{124{,}696} \end{array}$$

5. **(A)** $\dfrac{8}{27} \times \dfrac{9}{16} = \dfrac{1}{3} \times \dfrac{1}{2} = \dfrac{1}{6}$

6. **(C)** $\dfrac{34}{60} - \dfrac{27}{60} = \dfrac{7}{60}$

7. **(B)** $\dfrac{41}{5} \times \dfrac{2}{1} = \dfrac{82}{5} = \mathbf{16\dfrac{2}{5}}$

8. **(D)**

$$\begin{array}{c|c} IS & 5 \\ \hline 18 & 100 \end{array} \qquad \begin{array}{l} 18 \times 5 = 90 \\ 90 \div 100 = \mathbf{0.9} \end{array}$$

9. **(A)** $\dfrac{4}{3} \div \dfrac{8}{9} = \dfrac{4}{3} \times \dfrac{9}{8} = \dfrac{36}{24} = \dfrac{3}{2} = \mathbf{1\dfrac{1}{2}}$

10. (C)
```
   3.30
    .46
+ 88.00
  91.76
```

11. (D)
```
   8.6
x  2.1
   86
  172
 18.06
```

12. (B) The product of 7 x 3 is 21. Each number has two decimal places for a total of four in the answer **.0021**.

13. (A)
```
  38.15
 -21.70
  16.45
```

14. (B)

IS	60
95	100

$95 \times 60 = 5700$

$5700 \div 100 = \mathbf{57}$

15. (D)
```
       970
0.4)3880
    36
    28
    28
     0
```

16. (A)

16.17	%
46.2	100

$16.17 \times 100 = 1617$

$1617 \div 46.2 = \mathbf{35}$

17. (C)
```
  102
x  98
  816
  918
 9996
```

18. (D)
```
     11
21)231
   21
   21
   21
```

19. **(C)**

63.2	40
OF	100

$63.2 \times 100 = 6,320$

$6,320 \div 40 = \textbf{158}$

20. **(C)**

IS	0.3
103	100

$0.3 \times 103 = 30.9$

$30.9 \div 100 = \textbf{.309}$

Following Directions

1. **(D)**	6. **(B)**	11. **(D)**
2. **(C)**	7. **(B)**	12. **(D)**
3. **(A)**	8. **(C)**	13. **(B)**
4. **(A)**	9. **(C)**	14. **(B)**
5. **(B)**	10. **(D)**	15. **(C)**

Number Groups

1. **(C)** The last numbers are even. 8885 is different because it is odd.

2. **(D)** All numbers are consecutive descending. 6789 is different because it is consecutive ascending.

3. **(B)** The sum of the outside pair of digits equals the inside digits. 8145 is different because 8 + 5 is equal to 13 not 14.

4. **(C)** All numbers begin with 25 and the last two digits are greater than 25. 2523 is different because the last two digits 2 and 3 are less than 25.

5. **(D)** All the numbers are even except for 6007.

6. **(A)** The product of the first 2 digits is equal to the last digit. 2202 is different because 2 x 2 does not equal 2.

7. **(D)** The sum of the first 2 digits is equal to the last 2 digits. 8716 is different because 8 + 7 = 15 not 16.

8. **(A)** The last pair of digits in each number is 00. 0011 is different because 00 is the first pair, not the last pair.

9. **(C)** Each number is an arrangement of 3, 3, 3 and 0. 3030 is different because there are only 2 threes, and 2 zeros.

10. **(A)** Each number repeats the same digit except for 1444.

11. **(D)** Each number is an arrangement of the digits 8, 7, 3, 2. 3875 has a 5 instead of a 2 needed for this arrangement.

12. **(A)** Each pair of digits in each number have a difference of one.

13. **(B)** All the numbers are odd. 3320 is the only even number.

14. **(D)** Each number is an arrangement of the digits 2, 4, 6, 8. 4680 has a zero instead of a 2.

15. **(C)** Each number is a pair of repeats. 1123 needed to be 1122 to follow the common pattern.

16. **(D)** The zeros in each number are in the second and fourth positions. 0404 has zeros in the first and third positions.

17. **(D)** The sum of all the digits in each number is 15. The sum of the digits in 3427 is 16 not 15.

18. **(C)** The inside repeating numbers are one more than the outside repeating numbers. 3223 is different because 2 is one less than 3.

19. **(B)** All the numbers begin with an odd digit. 4000 is the only one beginning with an even digit.

20. **(D)** The first two digits make a sum of ten. 4755 is different because 4 + 7 = 11 not 10.

Spelling

Check Spelling list for correct spelling.

1. (A)	6. (C)	11. (D)	16. (A)	21. (B)	26. (B)
2. (C)	7. (B)	12. (A)	17. (D)	22. (C)	27. (A)
3. (B)	8. (D)	13. (C)	18. (A)	23. (A)	28. (C)
4. (C)	9. (D)	14. (B)	19. (D)	24. (B)	29. (C)
5. (A)	10. (A)	15. (B)	20. (A)	25. (D)	30. (D)